PERIOD COSTUME
FOR THE STAGE

PERIOD COSTUME FOR THE STAGE

Tina Bicât

The Crowood Press

First published in 2003 by
The Crowood Press Ltd
Ramsbury, Marlborough
Wiltshire SN8 2HR

www.crowood.com

British Library Cataloguing-in-Publication Data
A catalogue record for this book is available from the British Library.

ISBN 1 86126 589 1

Dedication
For Trish McDonnell and Jessie Caujolle.

Acknowledgements
Affectionate thanks to Kate Bicât for organizing and checking the illustrations, Trish
McDonnell for looking and listening, Gwyneth Powell and Alan Leith for the cover illustration,
Robin Brodhurst for his clear look at my idea of history, Polly McDonnell for her help with the
index and of course, Gerard Boynton and the staff and students of St Mary's College at
Strawberry Hill.

Photograph previous page: Costume from the rag-bag. A London street vendor wearing
armour home-made from old clothes, rags and belts. Photograph by Hannah Bicât.

Typeset by Jean Cussons Typesetting, Diss, Norfolk

Printed and bound in Great Britain by Biddles Ltd, Guildford and King's Lynn

CONTENTS

THE TEN-MINUTE TOUR 6

INTRODUCTION 9

1 BASIC COSTUME 14

2 CRUSADERS AND TROUBADOURS 1066–1485 21

3 THE DARK AND DAZZLING TUDORS 1485–1603 33

4 LINEN, LACE AND CIVIL WAR 1603–1660 44

5 CULTURE, CURLS AND THE COUNTRY HOUSE 1660–1789 54

6 JANE AUSTEN AT HOME AND REBELLION ABROAD
     1789–1840 65

7 CORSETS, COMMUNICATIONS AND QUEEN VICTORIA
     1840–1900 76

8 FROM DRAWING ROOM TO BATTLEFIELD 1900–1945 88

9 A WORLD IN THE LIVING ROOM 1945–2000 103

10 PATTERNS, MODIFICATIONS AND SUBSTITUTIONS 114

APPENDIX – USEFUL TIPS FOR COSTUME MAKERS 135

BIBLIOGRAPHY 139

INDEX 140

The Ten-Minute Tour

THE PEOPLE OF BRITAIN AND THEIR CLOTHES

Saxons: draped, plaited and girdled at home, or marching armed with leather and painted with woad through the early centuries. The Normans conquer in their chain mail and helmets. The knight sets off to the crusades, his lady's sleeve or glove fluttering as he gallops. Then on, through the rough-jewelled collars and belts to the shaping and decoration of the fifteenth century, cutting more elaborate figures with patterns and pleats, scollops and dags, folds and plenty. The start of the long march of the waist. The exodus of the neck for women, and men showing a leg from choice, rather than economy or practicality. Women must breed and strengthen Britain. Clothes display a more varied choice of cloth, cut and decoration.

Oh, it's all happening here. People are travelling more; books are coming out of monasteries, and pictures out of churches. The Middle Ages end, and those ramping Tudors, all male in power and shoulders, display the symbols of wealth and education. Shakespeare was here, which changes everything for us, but not for them. Big sleeves, big jewels and big egos. Waists down for Elizabeth, up for Charles I. Off with his ribbonned and curled head, and sober Cromwell squashes down the frills.
But only for a few years. Up they flourish to welcome Charles II. Silks and satin sweep eighteenth-century court and country. Bosoms out and in, everyone who could afford it peacocking about, and the fashion show we know today from magazines kicks in – only instead of at the bookstall on the station, it is displayed in the moving tableaux of court and high society. Afloat on a zipping and turbulent current. Restraint and reckless extravagance exist side by side. Exquisite elegance and intellectual gymnastics. Ruffles, frills, satins and brocades for both sexes. Tiny feet and huge skirts. Men show off their elegant calves with a courtly bow. Hats and powdered wigs, and both sexes peer in the candle-lit looking glass to put on their make-up.

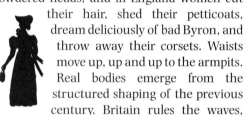

Across the channel in France, Madame la Guillotine lops off those bewigged and powdered heads, and in England women cut their hair, shed their petticoats, dream deliciously of bad Byron, and throw away their corsets. Waists move up, up and up to the armpits. Real bodies emerge from the structured shaping of the previous century. Britain rules the waves, not only at Trafalgar, but also in ships full of imported cloth and dye and exported fashion. Muslins and prints. Dresses that can be washed. Snowy linen for men and the start of the sober suit, though Beau Brummel spends hours with his valet adjusting his cravat. Modest bonnets, and dresses that reveal the body apparently by mistake. Male thighs demand attention, but not as much attention as the exquisitely tied neckwear. Every nice girl loves a soldier, and the not-so-nice dampen their muslins to make them cling to the thigh. Waists move down, down, down.

Sleeves and skirts start to burgeon again. Queen Victoria and modesty clamp in on the little woman, and the corset prevails. Women's bodies don't exist below the waist; even piano legs wear skirts, and trousers are less tight over the hips. The difference between man the provider and decider, and woman the acquiescent breeder, is very marked. Wide crinolines and high top hats. Yards of cloth in skirts over wadding of petticoats. Waistcoats, bonnets and the cravat. Skirts begin to narrow. The emphasis creeps round to the unmentionable bum, and the bustle begins. Men's clothes reveal less and less of their body shape, and women's curves are emphasized by the bustle and the burgeoning bosom, which make the tight-laced waist look even smaller. The century turns, Victoria dies, and the hour-glass figure is at its most curvaceous and provocative, though covered right up to the neck, just like the morals of its society.

The pace of invention really starts to speed up, as communications improve. Fashion magazines, trains and travel. Men, when not in uniform for World War I, change slowly and with some subtlety, but women take fashion flight as peace is declared. The old guard reel at the sight of the first peeping ankle and at voting women, and as soon as they have recovered from that fit of the vapours they are

assailed by the 1920s knee covered in a light and often flesh-coloured stocking.

Beads and legs flash in a wild Charleston between the two great sad wars. Respectable women flatten their busts and wear make-up. Again the necessity for fecundity – all those dead young men among the poppies: and the survivors put on their soft-brimmed hats, shrug into wide-bottomed trousers and Fair Isle, and kiss the lip-sticked girls. And everyone sees it, on newsreels, on films and in papers, and so it echoes throughout the classes. Women, after their tomboy phase, long for glamour, and slither, bare backed, into the 1930s, or borrow the beautiful tailoring of their elegant men and smoulder in a daring cloud of cigarette smoke.

War, terrible war, again. Men in uniform, and women too, when not in the economical Rational Dress advised by government. The catwalk and the Women's Institute meet over the ration book, and boil the contour lines off old linen maps of the Empire to make blouses and baby clothes. Peace at last: as rationing retires, a swish of skirts leads us back to the small-waisted, curvy 1950s' woman and to man the provider, solid in his square-shouldered jackets.

Fecundity again – bigger hips are 'in' after the war. A huge gulf opens between the generations and their clothes. The wild release of Youth rocks through the sixties, pointed

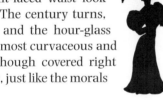

bras then flat chests, very short or very long skirts. Casually dressed men, freed from the necessity to be overtly male because of the post-war population explosion, grow their hair, and flower power, denim and the contraceptive pill take fashion back to the peacock male and his glittering mate. Glam rock and punk and anyone of any generation wore the trousers. Power and money cut into the eighties, and the new Elizabethan woman echoes the earlier one with her powerful shoulders – though she shows her legs to the narrow-trousered man. As the millennium turns, young women bare their pierced bellies and reveal with confidence their bodies in Lycra, and men hide their hips in baggy trousers or cling to the 100-year-old suit. And as people's lives, through screens and papers, become more public, clothes become more body-concealing or deliberately revealing – and the changes roll on. Woman as waif, woman as leader. Woman as mother. Man strong and silent, man romantic, man the father. And so the romp in the ragbag rolls on, as it always has, and probably always will.

INTRODUCTION

Imagine you could hold a huge roll of cloth painted with the life of the centuries. Then imagine you could flap it, and it would unroll away from you for mile after mile, showing you pictures of people living their everyday lives in the past. You are holding the end of the cloth that shows our present life in clear, bright detail, with every mobile phone and trainer logo visible. Far away – small, smooth and heroic, across the sea in the distance of time – is William the Conqueror being waved off to war by his family. The detail may be obscured, but we can still see the glint of his chain mail and the scooped neck of the women's dresses. The rest we fill in from our imaginations and our certain knowledge that the deepest character and interest of men, women and children then was, at heart, much the same as that of men, women and children today.

CLASS AND STATUS

People use clothes and accessories to display their status to the world. Quite young children can decode the signs given by clothes, and by the time we are adult, we have all been practising understanding these significant messages for years. They have some odd rules, and the ability to decipher them can be, in itself, another message: accidentally or on purpose, we display so much about our individuality, interest and social situation with the clothes we wear. It is no accident that one of the first acts of a communist regime is to standardize the clothes of the comrades. Even when uniforms follow strict rules people will still manage to give out clues with just the tiniest alteration of their costume. A group of teenage children coming out of school, all in a similar uniform, will have made tiny variations to their ties and skirt lengths, which display an instinctive awareness of fashion and an urge to display their individual character.

The earl in his garden may well be wearing the same frayed, muddy, patched clothes as a tramp, but the message he gives out is of nonchalant assurance rather than stricken hunger. It's all in the way he – or in theatre's case, the actor – wears the clothes. Similarly, how do we know that the ripped and faded jeans that are a fashion statement, are not the ripped and faded jeans of the vagrant? Why do

the boys at the most prestigious and expensive schools in England wear clothes that went out of fashion before World War I? Why do barristers wear wigs, and academics wear Tudor gowns? Why do we pay extra to advertise someone else's business name on our accessories? If nobody could decode the signs, there would be no point in them. We have to understand the rules – and that, in itself, gives a message; or ignore them and wear what we like, and that's another message.

This isn't new. Clothes have always been used by men and women as a sign language to advertise their character, status and sympathies. When using these signs to help tell a story to an audience, it isn't the historical accuracy or cleverness of a costume that gives most of the audience clues they can decipher; it's showing them signs they can recognize. It may be correct to put a four-year-old Tudor boy in a skirt, but to most people in the audience he will look like a girl; there is absolutely no point in that sort of application of research.

Work Clothes

The development in communications – particularly with regard to photographs in newspapers and magazines, and the television in most homes – has made it much easier to visualize the clothes worn by people in all walks of life. It can be difficult to research working clothes of earlier times, as the poor led less well documented lives than the rich. Thus the king's crown will survive, but the shepherd's hat is lost in the mud, and Mrs Shepherd hadn't the money to have his portrait painted. Indeed his portrait, if it *were* to survive, is likely to present a romanticized version of the real thing and be painted for a noble drawing room, rather than to decorate Mrs Shepherd's humble cottage.

The most useful research may prove to be in imagining how the basic styles of the day would have been adapted for working use. The maid might have inherited her ground-length skirt from her mistress, but she must tuck it up to keep it out of the mud, wear an apron to protect it from the ashes and roll up the sleeves so they don't dangle in the washing-up water. What would you do if you had to dig in the rain and had no coat? If you went shrimping in a long skirt? Had no trousers for your little son? Wanted a pretty new hat and had only an old one and no money? If you can imagine yourself solving these problems in the time you are researching, you will probably come up with the same answers as the people did then.

The different classes might have tried to follow the styles of wealthy society, but fashions always change more slowly and are less extreme when time and money are wanting. Poverty means less cloth in the garments, fewer accessories, and more mending, altering and patching.

How the Book Works

The magazines of today and the portraits of yesterday present a clear-edged version of a blurred picture, and give us a peculiar view of fashion. If you compare a random group of people crossing the road with a few pages torn from the latest issue of a fashion magazine, you will find few similarities. Many men and women will be wearing clothes that would not have looked out of place half a century ago; indeed, the contrast in the way people dressed, and the variation of style, must always have been as great as it is in any street scene today.

When studying the script before designing costumes it is essential to chart the relative status of the characters in the play. Society in general has always been obsessed with class and status, and any designs for historical drama must demonstrate an understanding of the class structure of the time. Clothes display,

Written descriptions of a character can produce a sparkling visual image:

He wore ... a decent hat with binding round the edge, the hat worn brown and glossy; his shoes were small, thin shoes, pretty good. They had belonged to a gentleman. His coat was blue, frock-shaped, coming over his thighs. It had been joined up at the seams behind with a paler blue, to let it out, and there were three bell-shaped patches of darker blue behind, where the buttons had been. His breeches were either fustian, or grey cloth, with strings hanging down, whole and tight. He had a checked shirt on, and a smaller coloured handkerchief tied round his neck. His bags were hung over each shoulder, and lay on each side of him, below his breast. One was brownish and of coarse stuff, the other was white with meal, on the outside, and his blue waistcoat was whitened with meal.

From Dorothy Wordsworth's *Journal* (Macmillan & Co Ltd, 1801)

in the most convenient way, signs that can also be given with cars, houses, accents, manners and education, and this puts the costume designer in the enviable position of being able to use a language that nearly everyone understands.

This book is written from our contemporary perspective, and will look through our eyes at the past. It accepts the idea that historical accuracy is impossible to recreate because the eyes that look at the actors onstage are the eyes of today. We would probably vomit at the smell in the most refined Jacobean dressing room, and the historically accurate knight in shining armour would grate our fleabites in his rusty and clanking embrace. The theatre designer must adapt to current sensibilities so that we, today's lovers, recognize the passionate avalanche of Juliet and Romeo, and, as today's sportsmen, the tension and skill of the tournament.

Women lead fashion with inventions as dazzling and fugitive as a butterfly's wing, and the men follow on behind. The ideal of feminine beauty is notoriously changeable, and a realistic Mr Darcy would cut no ice with today's Miss Bennett. The picture we paint has to give the right message to today's audience.

Young men and women have always shocked and enraged their elders with fashions that seem designed to challenge the conventions of the time. Today's piercings and tattoos continue a trend as old as Adam and Eve's fig leaves. However, these exaggerations are so many and so fleeting that they have been largely ignored here, as they need a whole book of their own.

Historical costume, with its complications of cut, corsets and coat tails, is a skilful and very expensive procedure. But there is another way, and with an informed and open mind, and an understanding and clear picture of the people of the period you are trying to recreate, you can invent a picture of life in the past that the audience will recognize.

The book begins with a chapter about basic costume. It is important to grasp the principle of how to make and use it, and how to combine it with particular signs and significant accessories and adaptations in order to clothe actors in period plays. Then read the chapter that includes any date that interests you, and you will understand the way the book works. Each chapter demonstrates particular ideas and will lead you to further research should you want a more traditional result – or, as will probably happen, you are caught up in the excitement of inventing your own ideas that suggest the period.

Exaggerations of costume through the ages.

The book is arranged more or less century by century, starting in the eleventh, and ending in the year 2000. Should history and costume dictate another, more appropriate division, the book will follow: for instance, the Battle of Waterloo works better as a division than 1800. More space is given to the centuries nearer our own, as fashion changes more quickly as communication accelerates. The final chapter is a collection of ideas, simple patterns and practical information that will help when costuming a period play. It gives a practical demonstration of some useful and very adaptable patterns, and shows simple ways to achieve the effects you want. Many of these can be adapted to very different periods. Note that the hundreds of technical words that have been used over the centuries to describe the different garments have been avoided wherever possible, and replaced by a modern equivalent.

This book aims to demonstrate, in a way that is comprehensible and practical, how to use basic costume and modern clothes to suggest the feeling of a period in the past. It will show methods useful for conventional production, and suggest effective methods for post-modern deconstruction, or a more abstract physical theatre. Each chapter starts with a condensed view of life in those times, and its clothes. There is no limit to the amount of further information that can be discovered about any of these times. These guides to the times and the social behaviour of our ancestors help to place the play and the costume in a historical frame, and help you invent costumes that will give the right message to the audience.

The ideas for representative costumes that appear in each section will not necessarily correspond with the fashions of that era – they will suggest a style that might be appropriate to the time. Many plays can be set in a different era when perhaps the political or social situations have a sympathetic relevance, so it's worth thumbing through the centuries before settling on a specific period. The bibliography at the end of the book will introduce you to books where you can find a more accurate guide to the placing of seams and the mysteries of corseting, and all the other techniques used by professional historical costume designers and makers.

The quotes that follow are chosen from books that give today's reader a particular insight into the life and manners of men and women in the past. Reading their contemporary literature rounds out the visual image

A medieval housewife, Margaret Paston, opens a window in a wall of time five centuries thick, for us to hear the scratching of her pen as she writes to her husband to bring her '... some cross-bows and wyndacs (grappling irons) and quarrels (cross-bow bolts)' to defend their house; in the same letter as she asks for '... one pound of almonds and one of sugar ... and some frieze' (woollen cloth) to make of your child his gowns.

From *The Paston Letters* (G. Bell & Sons)

given by the other arts, and helps us understand the lives of the people who wore the clothes and the message they gave to the people of the time. History was the present when they wrote, and their stories, with freshness and clarity, show us their thoughts, emotions and attitudes.

FINDING INSPIRATION

Music

We may not be able to smell the past, but we can still hear it, and the music of the past makes it possible for us to inhabit the souls and walk in the bodies of our ancestors in a way that no words can. Find and listen to music written and performed in the period you are researching: its rhythms, and its songs and dances, will feed you with the spirit of the time. This is not a fanciful notion – it is practical fact. A song may conjure up your own past more vividly than a photograph.

Visual Art

Painters, sculptors, cartoonists and illustrators recorded the lives of their fellow men, and in the last century, film makers and photographers joined these recording angels. The pictures they have left us of their world demonstrate how their ideas of beauty, class, power and poverty differed from ours. The examples in the table below have been chosen because their work seems to reflect the look of the people of the time, and to give an insight into the social and moral climate of their world. They are merely a nudge towards the profusion of riches in each category, and are an arbitrary and personal choice.

Chapter 2	1066–1485	The Bayeux Tapestry and the Luttrell Psalter
Chapter 3	1485–1603	Hans Holbein and Nicholas Hilliard
Chapter 4	1603–1660	Van Dyck and William Dobson
Chapter 5	1660–1789	Sir Godfrey Kneller and William Hogarth
Chapter 6	1789–1840	George Morland and David Wilkie
Chapter 7	1840–1900	William Powell Frith and James Abbott McNeill Whistler
Chapter 8	1900–1945	John Singer Sargent and Walter Sickert
Chapter 9	1945–2000	Lucian Freud and David Hockney

A nudge towards some of the many works of art which capture the spirit of their time.

1 BASIC COSTUME

Many of the ideas for costume in this book will be used in conjunction with a basic costume, so it seems sensible to begin with an explanation of its purpose, how to create it, and how to use it. The audience buy their tickets and sit in their seats fully aware that what they have come to see is a performance, and not real life. Basic costume, and the way it is used, depends on this agreement, this willingness to believe. The designer must stir the imagination with visual hints that will guide the audience to imagining the correct period, situation and class of each character.

WHAT IS BASIC COSTUME?

Basic costume uses clothes that are non-character specific, as a background for accessories and detail, and it is these that give the idea of character, place and time. The possibilities and variety in designing this base are limited only by the need for it to have the chameleon-like ability to change its nature in different circumstances. Thus it could be as simple as black trousers, shirts, socks and shoes for the whole company, or it could mean all the company being dressed in cream linen, the men in Tudor doublet and hose, and the women in elaborately cut Elizabethan dresses with farthingales. The roads that lead to the decisions you take, begin at several different gateways.

What Style or Genre?

It is imperative to understand the style or genre of the work before producing ideas. Basic costume lends itself to a non-naturalistic style. It can be used in a naturalistic production, but only if it doesn't jerk the audience's belief out of true by being outlandish, or by drawing particular attention to itself. A work set in a period when corsets and elaborate wigs were in vogue, but which uses a physical style of performance, might not benefit from the restrictive style of movement imposed by period costume; it could prevent the actor from moving in the abstract way the director or movement director might wish. The sight of an actress playing the cello whilst wearing a huge Tudor farthingale is comic, rather than passionate, and it might be better to suggest the period with a more accommodating, albeit less accurate, long skirt and a ruff. The designer must invent a visual representation of a character. This may not be historically accurate, but it should create a costume which, combined with all the other elements in the picture onstage, creates a view of another era.

When the piece is a deconstruction of an existing text, the designer has to understand the perspective of the director as well as that of the subject matter, and create a costume that relates most particularly to the feeling being created. The subject may be a Shakespeare play, let us say *Macbeth*, which demands a heavy and realistic type of costume and arms. The deconstruction may revolve round the influence of the supernatural on the rational mind, bringing the three witches and the ghosts forward as major protagonists in an emotional and perhaps twenty-first century struggle. Macbeth, Lady Macbeth and their eleventh-century dilemmas might recede to take a minor place in the action. In such a situation, when a twenty-first-century witch might be looking up her spells on the Internet, eleventh-century costume would be ridiculous. It is a designer's job to understand and support the director's vision with visual means.

CHOOSING THE DESIGN FOR THE BASIC COSTUME

The primary source of inspiration is the content of the performance. This may be a script, or it may be a novel, an event, a poem, or any one of the many stimuli that lead humans to create a performance. Research of both the actual content and its surrounding area is the first step of the journey. As this research progresses and your knowledge of the subject matter expands, a picture of the people connected with that research will grow in your head, not merely their clothes, but the way they live, love, have breakfast, chat, govern and die. The purpose of the research is to understand the humanity of those whom you are going to dress as individual, breathing people in the world created by script, director, set designer and actors. A costume designer works with one limitation, and one that must override all others: the people who wear the clothes are humans and must perforce remain so, even if they appear before the audience as an aeroplane, or thunder, or a pantomime horse's rear end.

A Tight Budget

It can cost a great deal of money to clothe actors in historically accurate costume, and the expense of the actual clothes is only a proportion of the whole cost. This may include wigs, gloves, shoes or boots, weapons, costume props and all sorts of other items. A designer on a tight budget may find that basic costume is the best way to cope with the demands of a period production. Those needing to recreate complex costume on a limited budget need every ounce of imagination, and a particularly clear grasp of the essence of the characters in the play, and their situation within the piece they are to design and dress.

Identity Through Colour

A basic costume will most probably, but not invariably, be neutral in colour. Definite colours, such as reds or yellows, tend to lead the audience to assumptions about the people dressed in them. For instance, a woman in a scarlet dress will create an impression of a vivid, emotional, perhaps passionate and dangerous character. A woman in a beige, stone-coloured or grey dress can demonstrate the same emotional mood with the addition of a scarlet scarf or shoes. But adding a beige belt to a red dress would not alter the audience perception one jot.

Below is a table demonstrating some neutral colours and some definite ones; also some very basic suggestions regarding accessories that will alter the way the audience understands the message the costume displays. Think of the actors dressed in plain tunic and trousers, or a skirt of the 'neutral' colour, and then either imagine them, or draw them, with the 'definite' colour accessories. The sort of characters that come into your head will show you how easy it is to give different messages to the audience in this way.

The examples in the table on page 16 demonstrate this idea. The colour combinations you use might be more subtle, and they might involve a contrast of texture, rather than colour. They might involve several accessories, overskirts or props for each character. When you understand the principle, and begin to work with it, it will become clear that there are few limits to the information you can transmit.

Neutral colour of basic costume	Definite colour of accessories	Simple accessories: adding definite colour to a neutral base
Black	Red	Large chiffon stole
Brown	Burnt orange	Apron with bib
Buff	Yellow	Jester's hat and stick
Stone	Green	Circlet and wreaths of leaves
Grey	Blue	Collar, hair ribbons and rag doll
White	Purple	Elaborately decorative sash
Cream	Gold	Crown, orb and sceptre
Beige	Silver	Huge glimmering cloak

Colour and basic costume.

The Significance of the Silhouette

The choice of the *shape* of the basic costume is one of the most direct ways to lead an audience to the right era. Throughout the chapters in this book you will find silhouettes of figures contemporary to each period, and these will demonstrate just how much the outline tells us.

The silhouette is vital if a suggestion of the past is important to the piece on which you are working. You will have great difficulty in fostering a belief in Queen Victoria without the bell shape of a long skirt, or in Henry VIII without his square short doublet. This does not mean that historical realism is necessary for the audience to believe the actors are people from the past. The bell-shaped skirt could be made out of net, through which the trousers and top of the basic costume can be seen; and the square-shouldered doublet could be a coat cut in thick blanketing and worn over ordinary trousers. Thus it doesn't have to be real – but it does have to be acceptable, both as a modern garment and to suggest a period.

The silhouette of the head – its hat, hairstyle, beard and moustache – is another useful pointer: could you imagine a 1920s' flapper with her hair flowing round her

shoulders, or Santa Claus without his beard? Again, obvious examples. But it is remarkable how often we recognize people by their outline, rather than by their individual features. Try to lead your cast to a haircut or hairstyle that is right for the period.

Choosing the Right Cloth

The cloth used for the basic costume must be considered from several different angles.

- Colour: When combined with the other colours in the production, will it create the impression you hope for? Does it suggest the mood of the play, and the period?
- Texture: The way it hangs: the way it behaves when allowed to fall naturally – whether stiffly structured or flowing – can relate it directly to a particular era.
- Light: The way it reacts to light shining on it. Does it reflect the light in the way satin does, or absorb it richly like old sacks or velvet?
- Practicality: Will it be strong enough to withstand the rigorous demands of life on stage? Will it wash or clean well? Will it take dye or paint if you want it to?
- Cost: Can the budget afford it?

The Right Footwear

An actor's feet, and what he wears on them, are important. They always are – not only to the actor and audience, but also to the movement director and the sound department. Bare feet, particularly in a situation when a character would in reality wear shoes, are a sign to the audience that they must use their imagination in a different way than they would when watching a naturalistic play: a man in a suit with bare feet gives a very different message to a man in a suit shod in conventional shoes.

The shoes and the relationship of the style of shoe to the walk is, for many actors, a significant step in the development of their character. The feeling of their shoes and the sound of their footsteps stays with them when they walk away from the mirror at the fitting or in the dressing room, and supports them in their role throughout the performance. It is comforting for the budget-stretching costumier to remember that people with less money have always found boots and shoes an expensive problem. The finish of a stage shoe – dusty, polished, patched or shiny – is full of information for the audience about the character and status of its wearer. Every effort should be made to provide the right footwear early enough for the actors to rehearse and get used to the shoes they will be wearing on the first night.

In a situation where there is likely to be a particularly physical slant to a performance, the sort of movement should be discussed with the movement director, as well as in individual discussions with the actors. Many sets can be inconvenient or even dangerous for barefoot actors, and the subject should be raised at an early production meeting when both set designer and movement director are present. It is much better to sort any problems out in advance than have people staying up all night before the technical rehearsal covering splintery scaffolding planks with painted carpet.

THE USE OF PROPS

Traditional theatre divides props into personal props (perhaps a dagger carried by the actor and usually kept in his dressing room), costume props (perhaps a handkerchief, provided by the wardrobe and kept as part of the costume) and stage props (perhaps a cup of tea, which is kept on the prop tables in the wings and collected as the actor goes onstage). When working with basic costume, the boundaries between costume and props become blurred, and often the accessory that gives the message most clearly to the audience is, in traditional theatrical terms, a prop rather than a costume. These props should be included in the costume design, as it is essential that they coalesce both with the basic costume and any other additions. For example, an adult in basic costume playing a little boy might be wearing a white collar and a straw hat and carrying a toy boat. The toy denotes his childishness. The boat, in this case, is part of the costume, and not an ordinary prop as it would be if he took it from a shelf onstage and ran off to play. Another example would be an actor playing the personification of a storm using a toy boat, where his physical movement created a picture for the audience of a violent tempest at sea: again, the boat could be considered part of his costume, and designed as such. These distinctions should be discussed in early production meetings, to make sure that everyone knows who is designing, making and budgeting for the boat.

All this chat about a toy boat may sound too exacting, but it is not. Every single item that appears onstage must be carefully considered and created to give the audience clear and intentional signs which they can decode.

Accessories, costume props, signs, symbols, signifiers, indexes or clues: all these words are used to describe the objects a designer uses to nudge the audience towards an understanding of the messages the costume designer is trying to convey. This book is primarily about creating a historical past. Even if nobody in the audience has studied costume or imagines

Basic costume	Example
Clothes of the same colour, but in different styles that suggest their separate characters	All in beige. Old man in mac and cloth cap; young woman in cotton sweater and linen trousers
Each character in a colour: top, trousers or skirt, tights or socks, shoes and all	Child in pale blue; grandfather in dark brown
White T-shirts and white trousers	The beggar torn, crumpled and dirty; the successful man gleaming white and ironed
Assorted dark suits, trousers or skirt and jacket; bare feet	The prince with shoes, waistcoat and smart accessories; the pauper with his trouser legs rolled up and his jacket inside out with the lining ripped out
Men in white vests and trousers; women in white sleeveless top and loose mid-calf-length trousers	Hair spiked with gel and armfuls of tattoos for the tough guy; hair down and shining and the glint of jewellery for the heroine

Some examples of basic costume that need further dressing with accessories or added costume items to relate to a specific period.

(Opposite) Some examples of basic costume related to particular era. These are suitable, with slight variations, for children as well as adults.

Era	Sex	Colour	Style	Head	Feet
Medieval	M	Brown	Loose jersey trousers and belted tunic	Hood with cowl	Soft boots
Tudor	M	Light grey	Full shirt with ruff, breeches, waistcoat with pepleum	Beret with narrow brim	Boots or pumps
Stuart	M	Black	Trousers or breeches, round-necked sweater, lace-edged collar and cuffs and sash	Small beard and moustache	Leather shoes
Civil War	M	Black	As above, with lace-edged or plain linen collar depending on allegiance	Hat with or without feathers	As above
Restoration and 18th Century	M	Beige and cream	White full shirt, breeches, stockings, lace cravat and cuffs	Tricorne hat	Shoes with decoration
Regency	M	Black and white	White high-necked shirt and cravat, black slim trousers	Regency-style top hat	Pumps
Victorian and Edwardian	M	Black	White, high-necked shirt, coloured soft bow at neck, straight-fronted waistcoat and slim trousers	Top hat	Chelsea boots
Mid-20th century	M	Dark	Suit, breeches, waistcoat, tie	Short hair	Lace-up shoes
Late 20th century	M	Denim and white	Jeans, vest or T-shirt	Natural	Trainers
Medieval	F	Brown	Ground-length tunic and girdle	Single plait	Pumps
Tudor	F	Light grey	Fitted waistcoat with peplum, full shirt over bum-roll	Half-moon head-dress	Pumps
Stuart	F	Black	Full, ground-length skirt, close-fitting round-necked top with wide, white lace-edged collar	Hair with side curls	Pumps
Civil War	F	Black	As above, with lace-edged or plain linen collar, depending on allegiance	White cap with or without frills	As above
Restoration and 18th Century	F	Beige and cream	Close-fitting, low-necked bodice, full length skirt with hip pads	Hair up with decoration	Shoes with rosettes
Regency	F	Cream or pastel	Ground-length, light tabard or stole belted under bust over slim, long skirt and close-fitting top	Bonnet	Pumps
Victorian and Edwardian	F	Black	Full, or shaped into bustle, ground-length skirt over leotard or closee-fitting top	Hair up in bun	Short boots with heel pumps
Mid-20th century	F	Dark	Calf-length skirt, well fitting blouse	Appropriately styled hair	Lace-up or court shoes
Late 20th century	F	Denim and white	Jeans, vest or T-shirt	Natural	Trainers

they know anything about it, their minds are full of half-forgotten information that can be resurrected with a bit of visual prodding. Think of a medieval princess: what springs to the front of your mind, and most other people's minds? A willowy lady in a flowing dress with perhaps one of those high, veiled conical hats. Think of a Victorian undertaker: what picture appears? A tall, thin man in a top hat and a frock coat. Try it with other characters, on a variety of people: an Elizabethan sailor; the gaoler taking a Roman traitor to the scaffold; a little girl doing her lessons in Jane Austin's house; death; Aids or the plague; fire; the Angel Gabriel. It is surprising how closely people arrive at a similar picture. The stretching and preciseness of this faculty is at the root of a successful use of basic costume.

The table on page 19 shows examples of basic costume related to particular eras: there are no rules – every play has different needs – and the table is merely a starting point for your own ideas.

It is possible, when the feeling of the play demands it, to create a much more bizarre impression. The men could be in army uniforms and the women in tutus – or the men in tutus and the women in army uniforms. Or the whole cast strapped into polythene and gaffer tape; or corsets and trousers; or bright yellow boilersuits and helmets. Your decision will be the result of extracting the essence out of the script and translating it into costume in a practical and manageable manner. The following chapters will suggest additions to these clothes that are particularly successful in suggesting each period. It is quite possible for an audience's imagination to be nudged so successfully that most of them will be unaware that the actors performing on stage are not in full historical costume.

2 CRUSADERS AND TROUBADOURS 1066–1485

THE LIFE OF THE TIME AND ITS CLOTHES

William the Conqueror, Duke of Normandy, was crowned King of England on Christmas Day, 1066 in a rather messy ceremony, when some of his supporters slaughtered others because they mistook cheers of support for roars of incitement to rebellion. This misunderstanding was caused, like so many disasters before and since, by a failure in communication: they didn't speak the same language unless they happened to speak Latin. Luckily for us, women in Canterbury, or possibly in northern France, were busily stitching away at the Bayeux tapestry. The embroidered horses and their riders clop along the country roads or thunder into battle, and send to us, across 1,000 years, a clear and lively record of those men and women and their moustaches and dresses, belts, helmets and leggings. This record, and illustrations and statues before and since, show us that the clothes of the people had not changed

dramatically for many hundreds of years before the Norman Conquest, and were not to do so for many years afterward. Cloth, mostly linen and wool, and leathers and furs were draped over the body, and the fitting achieved by girdles or belts. The belt of the king and queen might be heavy with gold and splendid with jewels, that of the poor man, a rough twisted cord or some knotted off-cut strips of sheepskin.

Saxon England became a province of Normandy. The reflection of ideas from across the Channel can be seen in the hundreds of Romanesque stone churches all over England, whose rounded, stocky arches continue to stand in our towns and villages; they formed the heart of the parishes, many of which still exist today.

Those pugnacious Normans landed in a country that was far from devoid of art and culture: we can still see relics of the Anglo-Saxon talent for pattern and decoration in the artefacts that preceded the Norman Conquest. We can be sure, too, that the pattern and

decoration in their manuscripts, jewellery and sculpture must have been used in the border decoration of their clothes.

It wasn't a peaceful coup. The barons, William's followers, who deposed most of the Anglo-Saxon landowners, were fierce fighters and jealous landlords. They built their cold castles like strongholds and ruled over much of the country, and those who worked their land had few rights, and led a hungry, muddy life. All England owed loyalty to the king in a pyramid of power: the freeholders and serfs as the wide base, serving the knights and the barons in the middle, who in turn served and fought for, the king at the peak. Much of England's forested land was an enclosed and exclusive hunting ground for the rich and powerful. It seems that when the Normans weren't fighting or building churches they were hunting, and ordering ears and hands to be lopped off any unfortunate peasant caught picking up firewood or poaching a rabbit on these lands.

Very few actual garments survive, but there are many descriptions and illustrations, and we can piece together a convincing, and

A song from 1150 shows us a familiar longing for shining jewellery, soft textures and pretty frivolities when times are hard and warlike:

Ser john geuyth me reluys ringes,
With praty plesure for to assay –
Ffures of the ffynest with other thynges:
I have no powre to say hym nay.

Roughly translated this means: 'How can I say no when you give me such lovely, pretty presents?' (*Secular Lyrics of the XIV and XV centuries*, ed. Rossel Hope Robbins, published Oxford Clarendon Press)

probably more or less accurate, picture from these sources. When attempting to re-create costumes from this time, a practical imagination combined with an understanding of what was acceptable, will fill in the gaps. We know more or less how the people of England lived at that time, and we can imagine the means that different classes had at their disposal when designing an impressive robe for a courtly occasion, or cobbling something together from anything that would keep out the cold. We can imagine how chain mail must have chafed and rubbed the skin, and how essential it must have been to wear a thick garment underneath that would protect the skin from damage. We know that even the grandest castles must have been cold, damp and smoky, that the rushes covering the floor must have harboured rotting ordure, and that the courtyard was a slurry of mud and dung. Surely those ladies – the ones we see glowing in their jewel-coloured, flowing dresses in illuminated manuscripts – must, in reality, have spent much of their times with their skirts tucked into their girdles to keep them from scraping in the muck.

The last of the Norman kings died half way through the twelfth century, and the first Plantagenet, Henry II, took the throne. The sturdy Norman churches that had seemed so rooted in the earth of England, began to change. The round arches began to point towards heaven in the beginnings of the more decorative Gothic style, a style that hooks out the vein of romance buried in most English hearts. The influence of these pointed, perpendicular shapes is evident in the people's clothes, which developed more elegant, flowing lines.

England started to settle down. By now, Normans and Anglo Saxons had intermingled, and the civilizing influence of Henry's legal reforms brought a more rational approach to the laws of the country. Trials were no longer conducted by ordeal or combat, and a common law began to be established. Henry's attempt to make the clergy subservient to this common law of England, and not to that of the Pope and Rome, was the root of the never-to-be forgotten quarrel that concluded with the murder of Thomas à Beckett. Henry's heirs used England as a moneybox until finally a revolt broke out, which forced the signing of the Magna Carta: this established the rights of the people of England and limited the power of the king.

These people lived in separate domains, with the castle and its lord and lady in the middle. The knights in shining armour, the gracious, chaste ladies, the romantic minstrels of the Age of Chivalry, have come to us newly polished by the gothic revivals that have been aroused by a particularly English love for the idealized thoughts they represent. The opposite – the barbarous tortures, the terrifying and bloody hackings and executions, and the constant threat of starvation and disease – are also clear in our minds, in the same brutal detail of extremes presented to us by the media of today. The reality, for most people most of the time, must have been a humdrum existence of seasonal food, seasonal pastimes and, for most, the simple labour necessary to keep themselves fed and housed. Most people wouldn't have seen a tournament, or heard of a battle until years afterwards, or met many people who lived outside their particular area. And most would have been unaware of the changes of fashion at court.

It is natural for us to wonder what the wives were doing whilst their men were galloping about the country brandishing swords, or were away for months or sometimes years at a time on a crusade. In fact the women would have become pretty adept at coping on their own, and protecting their property and their children from the unscrupulous. Presumably they had to manage the practical affairs of their families, estates and workers, with only an occasional greeting from their lords when some exhausted messenger turned up with news. Indeed there are records of many powerful women in the early centuries of the first millennium who governed lands and went crusading, and there must have been many more who are unrecorded. Any landowner away from home on one of the numerous calls to duty by the king would have reaped the benefit of leaving a reliable, educated and perhaps even literate wife at home in charge of his finances, home and possessions.

Throughout the turmoil and fighting, the intellectual life of England was expanding, and the stories and descriptions that men brought back from the crusades were stirring stuff. At home, learning came out of the monasteries and into the universities. Young noblemen and women were sent abroad to widen their horizons, and returned influenced by the courts of Europe. Art at this time was created for the glory of God and the bible, and its stories were the inspiration for the decoration of churches: most men and women were illiterate, and the visual illustration of religious themes was a picture everyone could understand. The azure heaven full of bright angels waiting for the good, and the black devils pitchforking the wicked into the flames of eternal torment, depicted a vivid truth on the church wall for both the unlettered and the educated alike. Images, not words, fuelled the imagination.

We can feel sure that, when the men returned from the crusades, they brought back cloth and trinkets for their wives and daughters as well as holy relics, the latter housed in gorgeous state and venerated in churches as an insurance against the devil and hell. Both trinkets and works of art would have given new ideas of pattern and fashion to the people of England. Many of the illustrations depict a romanticized life, and we need imagination and knowledge of humanity, just as much as factual research, to picture Everyman and Everywoman going about their daily lives.

We know that when women have time they will decorate their bodies and play with cloth (as will men, but more intermittently); indeed, they have done so throughout recorded time, since Adam and Eve covered their nakedness in the Garden of Eden and Penelope wove her tapestry in Ancient Greece. They probably always will. It might be guesswork, but we can feel pretty sure that, during those long days and weeks when their men were off fighting and crusading, the women were using their natural invention to create fashion. This, we know, involved more draping than tailoring, and it's a safe bet that the girdle that created and arranged those drapes, the length and style of the drapery, and the novelty and skill of mixing and setting dyes and embroidering decoration, would have employed much of their leisure. The travelling minstrel with his songs must have been grilled for information about clothes and cooking in other castles and counties, and been welcomed for his news as much as for his music and new songs.

A later version of the visual information of the Bayeux Tapestry in the twelfth century is conveyed in the lovely present of words Chaucer gave to us all in the fifteenth when he wrote the *Canterbury Tales*. Here, once again, we meet and recognize English men and women, and see them – in the same bright spring sunshine that shines on us – clopping along the road to Canterbury.

> A young man of the fifteenth century, curly-headed, broad-shouldered and fresh as May, whistles and sings as he rides ... 'Short was his gowne, with sleeves longe and wyde.' (Chaucer, *The Canterbury Tales* ed. Phyllis Hodgson, the Athlone Press)

The dynastic squabbles and long wars of the Middle Ages culminated in Bosworth Field, when the crown of England rolled off the dead head of the last Plantagenet king, Richard III, and was placed on the head of Henry, Earl of Richmond, who became the first of the great Tudor kings of England.

Clothes for Women

Heads and Headgear

Hair: At the beginning of the period, women's hair was long and worn loose or in plaits; by the beginning of the fourteenth century, hair was gathered into plaited mounds enclosed in decorative nets on the side or back of the head. Young women still in the marriage market and girls showed their siren hair to the men, but husbands and the church, which had a lot to say about the propriety or otherwise of various sorts of dress, insisted that wives should hide it, along with their other physical charms. Long hair could be plaited and coiled, or arranged on the head and covered with coarse nets made like miniature mobcaps decorated with beads. These nets could, of course, be stuffed with false hair if the natural hair was too short. Towards the end of the period the hair on the forehead and neck was plucked to accentuate the tall, perpendicular line of neck and face.

The veil: This progressed from a simple cloth over the natural hair, perhaps secured by a band round the head or draped under the chin, to a gauzy, transparent cover on the elaborate hats of the later years of the period.

The wimple: A linen cloth covering the throat and chin that was worn with a veil or headdress. To make this, gather the hair into a bun high on the back of the head. Drape a cloth under the chin, and secure into the bun on top of the head. Cover the hair and the join of the cloth with a veil. The shape, size and

CREATING THE CLOTHES FOR THE STAGE

Medieval women.

texture of the cloth, and the decoration of the top veil, can be varied according to the status of the character. The veil can be replaced with another band of cloth going round the head, or a padded roll or a hat.

The padded roll: Make a circle of a roll of wadding or thin foam, like a large doughnut, to fit the head. Cover it with fabric and decorate as appropriate. The roll can be used on its own, partially covered with a veil, or used like a coronet to hold the veil in place. A similar roll of a larger circumference may be shaped to form a more elaborate headdress, like the fat heart-shaped one of the fifteenth century. A 15cm (6in) piece of elastic on the inside at the back will make these headdresses sit more firmly.

The hennin: The fairy-story princess headdress. This miniature turret over a high, plucked forehead is shaped from a cone of stiffened material such as buckram, ending in a point or truncated to a sort of flowerpot shape. Hennins need to be light and sit very securely on the head. They are not the easiest style to use outside a fairy tale, as they look wrong if any hair shows at all unless the role has a fairy-tale princess's disregard for authenticity and her golden hair is allowed to tumble out. Fiddling about with a half circle of paper will show you how to work out a pattern.

Straw and felt hats: Simple, practical, round-brimmed hats for working people. These can be adapted from modern hats. A coarse straw will give a more authentic effect than a fine woven one. Modern felt hats can be reshaped and painted if necessary to look convincing. Remembering the simplicity of the means available to the medieval milliner will help you invent more authentic-looking styles for the different classes.

The bonnet or coif: A close-fitting cloth bonnet tied under the chin was worn by men, women and children alike, either under a hat or by itself. A close fit can be achieved without gussets if a very stretchy fabric is used.

Feet and Footwear
The fashionable medieval female foot, when not concealed by the gown, is slim and rather pointed, and the soft boots or shoes, sometimes held on with a strap, must have needed the protection of overshoes to cope with damp and dirt. Canvas ballet shoes or light, flat pumps dyed to match stockings will look right when glimpsed under the long skirt.

Covering the Body
Dresses: Most medieval female costume can be made simply by adapting and layering very basic shapes. A T-shaped, full-length smock with long, tight sleeves forms the underlayer – and for poorer women perhaps the only layer – of most women's dress of the period, and is a useful basic costume for the designer to add to. The overdress generally began as a wide-sleeved, unfitted tunic, often braided at cuff, collar and hem; this gradually became more fitted to the body, either with girdles or, later, by shaping at the waist by means of lacing or buttons. The oversleeves widened and lengthened, sometimes so much that they trailed on the floor and had to be knotted or tucked in the girdle. There was also an overdress with deep armholes that revealed the slim waist of the underdress beneath; this could have a decorative stiffened section at the front, and stiff encircling bands over the hips. Some dresses were so long that it was necessary to hold the front up high under the bust, or even tuck it into the deep armholes in order to walk, which accounts for the tipped-back posture seen in medieval illustrations. Undersleeves remained narrow, and skirts long and full throughout the period. The cut

became more complex, and the waistline shifted between hip and bust, or sometimes vanished completely.

The sleeves of this garment, which almost always show beneath the shorter or full sleeves of the overgarment, vary in cut and decoration: at different periods they were loosely fitted; very tight; cut long, and pushed in wrinkles up the forearm; finished with a little cone-shaped cuff that extended over the knuckles; buttoned from wrist to elbow; turned back, with cuffs lined in fur or contrast cloth; cut long, with a slit for the wrist to pass through, and dangling down over the under-sleeves; or finished with a wide band of decoration that sometimes gathered in fullness above the elbow or at the cuff. All were variations of the basic shift.

The layering of these clothes makes it easy to recreate or invent variations. For example, the lady of the castle could wear the T-shaped garment, quite closely fitted, under the sleeve-less tunic with a jewelled girdle gathering it round her hips. Her servant could wear nothing but a looser-fitting version of the same garment cut rather long and tucked up into a belt made of plaited strips of cloth. The differences in style can be created with belts and girdles, with the closeness or otherwise of the fit, and with texture and colour of fabric and its decoration.

The choice of fabric is vital. It must drape well without being flimsy, and ideally be slightly stretchy. If you hold the cloth up by

---

Margery, in 1477, suffering from the perennial problem of nothing to wear, writes to her husband: '... I have no gown to wear this winter but my black and my green-a-lyer, and that is so cumberous that I am eweary to wear it.' (*The Paston Letters*, G. Bell and Sons, 1920)

---

one corner and let it fall in its natural folds, you should be able to judge how it will hang on the body. Using cloth that stretches means that it will be easy to cut and fit a close-fitting garment without complicated darts, lacing or fastening. Many fabrics with a stretch- or a jersey-type weave do not fray, and will not have to be hemmed.

Cloaks: A rectangle of cloth with a cord or decorated band holding it across the chest.

Work Clothes

For poor women, the simplicity of cut that was apparent at the beginning of the period remained unchanged. Clever tailoring, that new invention, was for the rich; the poor just had to keep warm. Manuscripts and tapestries show the workers jollying about haymaking and weaving in fairly neat tunics; but again, the real picture must have been a haphazard bundle of layers kept together with belts or girdles.

Accessories

Headdresses, aprons, belts, cuffs, rings, girdles, collars, necklaces.

Clothes for Men

Heads and Headgear

Hair: The Bayeux tapestry shows us Norman William and his men with moustaches, and there are other references to facial hair. Since this was noticeable enough to be recorded at the time, and since for at least a hundred years after the Conquest it was easy to tell Normans and Anglo-Saxons apart whether dead or alive (there was a law that punished Saxons for a dead Norman, but not the reverse) we can assume that many of the men in power in the late eleventh and twelfth centuries wore facial hair. Small, trimmed moustaches and beards appear in illustrations. Hair was worn in an ear-length bob until, in the fifteenth century,

Medieval men.

the clean-shaven men cut theirs short at the neck and sides as if it had been cut round a crown.

Peasants' hair would have been longer and wilder, and roughly chopped or tied to keep it out of the eyes.

The bonnet or coif: For theatrical purposes this is best avoided on men, unless you want to raise a laugh or suggest old age. No modern audience could take a bonneted romantic hero seriously.

The hood: A useful, adaptable, and most practical garment that has been in constant use for thousands of years, and is still in use today. With rich cloth and scalloped edges to the cowl, and the hood lying back on the shoulders, it can be worn as an elaborate and lordly headdress. But imagine an old sack, split up one side to make a face-hole and up the back to allow the sacking to spread out to protect the shoulders, and you have a garment fit for the most wretched serf. Hats were sometimes worn over or under a hood. The hood could also be worn hanging down the back so that the whole garment became an extra, and often decorative, covering for the shoulders. The point of the hood could be extended, and either wound round the neck like a scarf, or looped up into the belt. It could also be worn as a hat, with the face hole round the crown of the head, and the spare cloth gathered up like a sort of turban. (If you try this out you will see how the liripipe hat developed and became so decorative.)

The cloth hat: Another adaptable shape, very like the pull-on knitted hats of today. This shape can be adapted for rich and poor by altering the length of the tube, and the size and decoration of the rolled-over section that forms the headband.

Felt or straw hats: These can be adapted from modern hats to create the floppy straw sun-hat of the ploughing peasant, Robin Hood's neat felt hat with a feather or to copy any of the styles in illustrations from the time.

Legs and Feet

Thick stockings or loose leggings covered the legs. Many illustrations show the feet in shoes that seem almost to be part of the hose. Boots and shoes follow the line of the foot, though they become more pointed as the centuries progress. Pattens (shoes on little platforms) were worn to keep the close-fitting, soft, flat shoes or boots out of the mud.

Shoes must have been as much of a problem to many medieval people as they are to the budget-conscious costumier. It is difficult to believe that these thin coverings afforded sufficient protection in the English winter. There is no real evidence of anything other than pattens or chain mail for protection, but surely some chilblained yeoman would have invented overboots or clogs to help combat damp and cold. Clumsy footwear such as straw bound round with crossed leather strips, or the rag-bandaged feet of the poor, can be created on the base of a gym pump or ballet shoe so that the actor can put the whole thing on like a boot. For theatrical purposes, when specialist theatrical footwear is not an affordable option, the best answer is to use the simplest and softest footwear available, or pumps disguised as cloth boots.

Covering the Body

The Tunic: Most male costume of the period, and particularly in the early centuries, is based on a T-shaped garment of varying length, richness and fullness. As the years progress, so does the shaping of this tunic, from the square-cut T-shape worn loose or with a belt, to the more fitted tunics of the fourteenth century. The cutting becomes more complex and precise, the closer fit demanding set-in sleeves and stitched pleats to shape the garment. A waist-length, close-fitting undertunic could be topped by a more elaborate and decorative version whose wide sleeves revealed the narrower ones beneath.

During this long period the length varied between ankle, calf, knee and thigh. By the fifteenth century, noblemen's clothes were more structured, and cut with a high collar. The shape of the sleeves of the overtunic altered with equal variety, though those of the undertunic remained long, neither men nor women showing their arms. The decorative oversleeves were cut in many inventive shapes: some ended with bands of decoration above or the elbow; some were cut as short oversleeves with long extensions at the back to hang down in points; some were cut over-long and worn pushed up the arm so that they wrinkled, but still ended up wrist length. Cuffs could be made with heavy decoration, buttoned and narrow, or widening to a tulip shape below the elbow. Sleeves could be scallopped, dagged or braided, and cut with a decorative slit at the elbow for the forearm to emerge in a contrasting undersleeve. All this variety based on a simple tunic of course provides much useful material for the costume designer to show status, character and period.

The tabard: This most simple garment, worn over an undertunic or chain mail, can be worn hanging loose, belted or half-belted (belt over the back, and the front hanging loose or vice-versa). It is an ideal canvas for the designer to decorate, and a useful cover to conceal short-comings in the undercostume. Because of its simplicity, extra care should be taken that it looks convincing: it must hang well, and not look flimsy or skimpy.

Tights and leggings: The leg coverings depend on the length of the tunic. They were, in reality and as far as we can judge, very varied in cut and closeness. Many were two separate legs joined only at the waist, which would be too revealing for most performances unless an appropriate-looking undergarment was worn. For some, today's thick and opaque tights would work. Leggings can be useful either cut off short under a working man's tunic, or long and tucked into boots for his master. They can be cut from stretch cloth to hook under the instep. A codpiece can be added and tied to points at the front.

The belt: This deserves a particular mention in this chapter, as the haversack of the day. Both the diagonal and waist belt of the time were used almost like an overnight case, a jewel box and a larder by medieval man. Quite apart from the rich and varied decoration of these belts, there are numerous illustrations of all sorts of items hooked onto the belt: cutlery, clothes, decorative medals, bones, mugs, instruments, water bottles and, of course, weapons, all dangle in a picturesque variety most useful to the costume designer. The jewelled belt of the nobleman was worn round waist or hips according to the fashion of the day. Belts were wide and buckled, sometimes decorated with jewels, long and pulled through a buckle to hang down in front or at the side, of sturdy plain leather with rough buckle, or made of metal plaques linked together, narrow or wide, with pouch attached.

The cloak: Cloaks were worn indoors and out for warmth and display. They could be short,

> In 1465 Paston writes from prison for his wife to send him: '... two ells of worsted for doublets, to happe me (wrap me up warmly) this cold winter'. (*The Paston Letters*, G. Bell and Sons 1920)

Useful ideas.

long, worn hanging from the shoulders and held in place by cords or a band across the chest, or draped under one arm. Some were hooded or collared, and some were lined in fur or in a contrasting colour and fabric. They were never lightweight or diaphanous. A wolfskin tied on to a hunter is a sort of cloak, as is the piece of linen used after the bath. A semi-circular or rectangular piece of cloth is an opportunity to demonstrate the status of the character, through the opulence of the cloth and its decoration.

Armour: Armour creates a problem for the low budget production, particularly as, if one person is armed, he tends to be surrounded by armed henchmen or attackers, or even a whole regiment, who must all be as convincingly and expensively equipped. Convincing armour is best hired or bought from experts. The old-fashioned stage chain-mail, hand-knitted from dishcloth cotton, dyed grey and painted, looked wonderfully convincing but is too labour-intensive a solution for today. Much, however, can be done to suggest a military idea to the audience with simple weapons and heraldic tabards.

Work Clothes
The quantity, colour and quality of cloth in a garment, as well as its decoration, was an indication of the status of the wearer. The poorest shepherd would have wrapped himself in one of his flock's skins and bound anything he could get hold of round his legs and feet to try to keep out the cold. The silhouette of the rich man was elegant and flowing, whilst that of the poor man was rough-edged and bundled. A plain, drab-coloured rough wool tunic belted with plain leather next to a richly coloured and decorated one belted with gold would tell a different story, even if the shape of both tunics was identical.

A loincloth can be made from a strip of cloth looped at back and front; worn with a rough tunic, this could form the dress of the working man.

Accessories
These include hats, hoods, gloves, belts (often with purses hanging from them), swords and daggers, a diagonal belt to hold the sword, or a bag in more peaceful times, jewellery round the shoulders like a mayoral chain today, or as a belt or cloak fastenings, rings, brooches as clasps.

Clothes for Children
Children were dressed more or less alike, in simpler versions of adult clothes. Boys had their hair cut, but girls' hair was long and loose. It can be easy for an audience to confuse the sexes of children onstage in costume of this period, and the difference should be clearer in the costume than it would have been in reality. Hoods, short hair, short tunics and belts for boys; and coifs, long hair and girdles for girls will help with their identification. Babies were swaddled into tight little bundles; in the case of noble infants, these could be expensively decorated.

Accessories
Hoods, coifs, belts, pouches, girdles, simple home-made toys.

Master Clement at School grew out of his gown as our children grow out of their school blazers. His mother writes that he '... hath a short, blue gown, that was raised (re-textured) and made of a side (long) gown when I was last at London'. (1458 Agnes Paston – *The Paston Letters* G. Bell and Sons, 1920)

3 THE DARK AND DAZZLING TUDORS 1485–1603

THE LIFE OF THE TIME AND ITS CLOTHES

Henry VII set to work on the chaos left by the Wars of the Roses. He filled England's coffers by taxing anyone who had anything to give, created and ruled over his Privy Council and the Court of the Star Chamber and squashed rebellions. In the relative peace that followed, educated and inquisitive people in England felt the heat of the Italian Renaissance. The world was expanding. Men looked for truth and a human perspective on life, and were not satisfied with an unquestioning acceptance of ecclesiastical teaching. Explorers discovered new lands, travellers told of the life and culture of other countries. Books could now be printed by the laity instead of being laboriously copied by monks, and the written word fanned the smouldering ideas into a vigorous blaze.

John Stow writes that when Henry VIII wore '... a round flat cap of scarlet (a sort of cloth) or of velvet, with a bruch (brooch) or a jewel, and a feather' that 'divers gentlemen, courtiers, and others, did the like'. (*The Survey of London*, John Stow, Dent, Everyman's Library, 1965)

Britain had been a little island more or less on the edge of world affairs. Now it lay proudly in its seas, gaining in power and establishing its place at the heart of the perspective lines so recently discovered in Renaissance Italy.

The son continued the pageant begun by his father – the great performance that wore its wealth on its sleeve and dazzled the senses with its display. For more than a century the overwhelming personalities of the Tudor dynasty displayed their power, the glory of

man and, most especially, the glory of the rulers of England – as in the sumptuous display to France at the Field of the Cloth of Gold. They understood the effect on people of outward show. They entertained wearing the most astonishing clothes, in rooms hung with glowing tapestries and glimmering with gold plate.

Henry VIII began his reign full of youthful energy with his coffers full of gold, his parks full of deer, his palaces full of music and good company, and his business affairs full of Cardinal Wolsey. Bluff King Hal was the English manifestation of Europe's Renaissance man: he hunted, sang, caroused and courted. Fashion, particularly male fashion, followed his roaring lead. The male silhouette expressed man's confidence in his strength and authority, with arrogance only equalled by the mythical superheroes of today. Clothes were heavy with decoration, crusty with jewels, stiff with gold thread, and sensual with fur.

Much of this personal decking to the glory of man was paid for with riches that had once glorified God. The rift with the Roman Catholic Church and the momentous change of England to a Protestant country led to the destruction of monasteries and the acquisition of their valuable belongings for the Crown.

Designers of fashion on the continent had used the discoveries of Columbus and Vasco da Gama to add new fuel to the fire of their imaginations. As England gained power it became less insular, and much of the fabric of the court's clothes was imported. The wealthy in England were dressed in silk from France, velvet from Italy, lace from Germany, and dyestuffs from the Indies – and of course wool, provided in abundance by England's sheep, particularly after Henry had enclosed and turned to pasture acres of common land, that once supplied a livelihood for the peasantry. The middle classes and workers wore wool or rough linen dyed with the readily available vegetable dyes grown in the countryside.

Men, not women, led fashion under Henry; but young Edward's reign redressed the balance, and brought the square outline and muscular shoulders in to more youthful and less macho proportions. Catholic Mary's brief and miserable time as queen tightened the silhouette still more whilst employing the gorgeous, if stiff and sombre decoration borrowed from the rigid courts of her Spanish husband.

And then Elizabeth – and female dress gradually displayed the power and strength of her England, with the queen herself, Gloriana indeed, hung with jewels like trophies of her triumphs. The long-legged men, their hips wide in padded breeches, and shoulders widened by epaulettes that emphasized the smallness of the waist, seemed to be imitating the female silhouette in homage to their queen.

Elizabeth's court spent huge amounts of money both on their rich costumes and the settings in which to display them. It was a display not only for the close inner circle, but also for the ambassadors from abroad and the common people. Elizabeth showed herself to her people in a series of carefully orchestrated parades. An exacting organization cleared the surrounding countryside of anyone likely to cause trouble, and stirred up interest and expectation in everyone else – and off she went, surrounded by her peacock court in a 'royal progress'. The gentry spent huge sums equipping, and in some cases even rebuilding, their houses and bankrupting their families for the honour of basking in the favour of being host to the queen and her retinue. This jewel box of a progress along the dusty roads must have seemed a glimpse of heaven to the ploughman in his buff wool tunic and the dairymaid in her coarse apron.

The Elizabethan world was a world of public spectacle and secret signs. Contemporary portraits and poetry are studded with messages for the eyes of the initiated. Beneath the polished screen of cold etiquette seethed a passionate, greedy, dangerous, poetic and deeply political river of intrigue and discovery. Her reign was a triumph of advertisement and propaganda. Four hundred years later the living picture she painted on her body – the mask-like make-up, the auburn wig and the rigid moulding of the stiff, opulent dresses – is the picture that kaleidoscopes to us through the centuries. We see her as the icon she created, the most important symbol in a time of symbols.

CREATING THE CLOTHES FOR THE STAGE

Clothes for Women

Hair and Headgear

Hair: Portraits tell us that hair was worn up, except in the case of young girls. But there are many literary references to flowing hair, which might foster a belief that the elaborately decorative hairstyles and hats were for formal and special occasions, and a less complicated hairdo was worn as a daily matter. We can be pretty certain, however, that whatever the style, a high forehead with no fringe was essential: no Tudor costume will look convincing with a fringe. A decorative band worn high on the hairline, particularly if of a light colour, will promote the feeling of the high plucked forehead that was in fashion at the time.

The hennin: The low hennin, shaped like a flowerpot with a veil, was in fashion during Henry VII's reign.

The hood: This wasn't a hood at all, but a structure like a neat little gabled house with a veil; it can be seen in many portraits of the early sixteenth century. Its particular use to the costume designer is that it covers the hair completely, unlike most Tudor headdresses. It is best constructed of thin foam on a skullcap base, because in this way the strict architectural silhouette can be decorated without becoming heavy and unwieldy to wear.

Hats: The different shapes of hat sat back from the hairline and tended to add height rather than width to the head of the wearer. Because most of the shapes are small and not head-hugging, make sure they don't slip back by sewing combs inside and perhaps by using back elastic concealed by the hair itself. A decorated skullcap can be created with strings of jewels attached, which can be twined and pinned into the hair when it has been styled.

The wreath: A simple and variable, if rather fanciful, option. Base the decoration of flowers or ribbons on a circle of wire or a small padded ring, which fits closely to the head.

The hairband: Another simple and effective option. A half-moon, stiffened shape that shows in the front and is secured by elastic at the back. Or a bought modern padded hairband enlivened with glued decoration.

Legs and Feet

Stockings don't show much, but if you need to make a point of them they were often coloured with elaborate clocks and knitted of cotton, silk or wool. Women's shoes were flat and rather broad-toed, and often highly decorated, and can be made by covering a flat court shoe or slipper with fabric

Clothing the Body

Dresses: Women's waistline settled in its natural position under a stiff bodice, which lengthened in front to a point over the stomach. The square wide neck and elaborate sleeves echoed the width of the male silhouette and rose, with theirs, to the high neckline of

Tudor women.

the later Tudor period. It is particularly interesting to note that by the time Elizabeth was established on the throne, the major difference between male and female costume was the fact that one had breeches on the bottom half and one had a skirt. The bodice shape was more or less the same, and somewhat asexual in cut. The skirts were wide and supported by stiffened petticoats, often with the added support of a padded roll just below the waist under the skirt. The extraordinary farthingale, like a wheel-shaped hoop under the skirt, created an outline as bizarre as a Martian's.

The clothes of these men and women are familiar to us from the portraits of Henry VIII and Elizabeth I and their courtiers. They have seeped into our historical vocabulary without us realizing. But imagine, for a moment, you are a woman actually wearing those clothes.

Your ribs are encased in a tight structure that comes high up into your armpits and is strutted at the sides to your waist. The front is rigid and presses over your stomach in a stiff point. When you sit down you must perch high on your buttocks or the point, stiffened with bone, wood or steel, will dig into your belly. Your arms must be held out from your sides because of the padding and decoration of your sleeves and the unyielding stiff sides of the bodice; besides, the rules of deportment have trained you to keep your elbows out to show the straight line of your upper body. Your neck is in its high stiff collar, perhaps stiff enough to mean you would have to hold your book up to read it, rather than rest it on the table, and a starched ruff itches your face and ears when you turn your head. Your body under its petticoats is bare except for your stockings and a padded roll round the back and sides of your waist. One of your petticoats holds a meter-wide hoop at waist level, tipped up at the back by the point of your bodice. All your clothes, except your cotton undershift, are very, very heavy.

To picture living wearing this sort of cage is to realize how few, how very few, of England's population wore these clothes; also, how more relaxed and unbuttoned versions of the basic shapes must have been common, even in upper-class situations. People dressed up in their best to be recorded by portrait painters for posterity. Those Tudor citizens who gaze at us from their portraits are as far from wearing their everyday clothes as a bride is when she changes her T-shirt and jeans for her white wedding dress today. How many proud parents today have photographs of their children dressed up for degree ceremonies wearing the hat and gown that would not have been out of place in a Tudor hall? It may appear to future generations that that is what all students wore all the time. Practical imagination must have as important a place in stage costume as historical research. Examples remain of a Tudor version of a long-sleeved knitted cardigan. Though this must have been a comfortable addition to the Tudor wardrobe, and historically correct wear, it would carry no message to the audience, as it bears no reference in its unstructured shape to the clothes they are used to seeing in portraits.

Katerina is tempted by Petruchio with the promise of '... silken coats and caps and golden rings, with ruffs and cuffs and farthingales and things!'. (*The Taming of the Shrew*, by William Shakespeare)

Undershift: A long-sleeved, full, washable cotton, linen or wool garment. This often showed by intention, through slashes, cuts or gaps in the top garments, as a decorative device. It could also show as a frill round the neck of a dress. It was used as a nightgown, and probably, with the addition of a bodice, formed

Lady Lisle is informed that in France 'Divers of the ladies hath their nightgowns embroidered, some with gold and some with silk'.(From *The Lisle Letters*, edited by Muriel St Clare Byrne, Penguin 1985)

the main dress of many of the lower classes. It can be made as a long and wide-based version of the tunic or the full blouse pattern.

Bum-roll: A stuffed cloth sausage tapering at the ends, tied with tapes round the waist to support the skirt at the back and sides.

Skirt: Ground-length, very full, and gathered or pleated into the waist.

Bodice: Close-fitting, stiffened and boned. The sleeves varied with the fashion throughout the era, but tended to be a significant part of the bodice; as well as carrying a great deal of decoration, they were complicated in cut and sometimes multi-layered. The decorative, trumpet-shaped gauntlets of gloves can give the impression of a cuff on a plain sleeve. A basic pattern for a boned corset could be adapted with sleeves and peplum to a Tudor shape, but it is a difficult thing for an inexperienced sewer to cut and fit. A close-fitting, long-sleeved body with an added ruff at neck and sleeves, or a stand-up collar, a full skirt over a bum roll, perhaps gloves with additions to the cuffs and a suitable headdress, will often look better than a dress that lacks the heaviness and extreme stiffness and perfect fit demanded by aristocratic costume of the time.

Cloaks and robes: Cloaks with hoods were the overcoats of the time, but a loose-fitting robe was worn both as a dressing gown and for extra warmth inside and out. For comfort, one imagines, as well as warmth, given the

extreme discomfort engendered by the formal clothes of the time.

Work Clothes
The shift – a long, full, T-shaped shirt – formed the base of working dress, with overskirts, bodices and aprons added according to the social position of the woman. The wimple or coif might be worn alone or under a hat, and a simple round-brimmed felt or straw hat worn instead of the more complicated and expensive headdresses of the wealthy. A look through a book of Tudor illustration, drawings and tapestries, as well as portraits, and a dip into the daily work of the character, will give you ideas for many more. A country woman in her garden might have a basket for collecting the eggs, an apron she could tuck into her belt to make a pouch to hold the chickens' food, a shawl tying her baby out of harm's way on her back and a wide-brimmed hat over a wimple to keep the sun from her eyes. A simple shift, perhaps belted over a bum-roll, would be all that was needed as background for these accessories. An actress in the same costume with a bunch of keys hanging from a chain at the waist, and a more formal hat over the hair rather than a wimple, would appear to be from a different social class.

Accessories
Ruffs, gloves, hats, fans, necklaces, rings, earrings and gems set within the embroidery of fabric.

Clothes for Men
Heads and Headgear
Hair: Hair was cropped, and moustaches and beards – first wide and full, and then trimmed and pointed – were worn.

Hats: These were worn indoors and outside, and echoed the silhouette of the clothes, beginning as wide and flat or rounded, and

Tudor men.

then adding height, rather than width, to the head. Plaited cloth rolls, brooches, feathers and plumes were used to embellish hats of the time, and wealthy people's hats were decorated with jewels and gold braid.

The flat hat: Like a beret with a small, stiffened brim. It is an extremely recognizable shape to an audience, as they are used to seeing it in portraits of Henry VIII.

The high-crowned hat: This had a small brim and a high crown, and can be made in much the same way as the flat hat, with height added by stiffening the cloth in the crown rather than letting it flop to the side. Feathers and quills tended to accentuate the vertical impression of these hats.

The skullcap-based hat: Use the crown of a modern felt hat as a skullcap, and cut the brim into flaps or scallops, or cut it off completely. Then you can turn up the re-cut brim to the style you want, and attach it to the crown of the hat with glue or stitches.

Legs and Feet
Shoes were flat-heeled and square-toed at the beginning of the period, and rounded by the end. They were made of cloth or leather, often decorated with slashes, jewels and embroidery, and for once present no particular problem to the costume maker as they can be constructed with thin leather or fabric on the base of a gym pump or plimsoll. Boots and half clogs that covered the toe were worn outdoors, or to protect the shoes.

Clothing the Body
The clothes of both men and women of this period seem to display the strong personalities of the Tudor monarchs. The more structured lines of the clothes that had taken root at the end of the Middle Ages, began to grow and

Officer's dress in the summer of 1590:
'Two shirts and bands, 9 shillings and 6 pence,
Two pairs of shoes, 4 shillings and 8 pence,
One pair of stockings, 2 shillings and eight pence
A felt hat and band, 5 shillings and 5 pence.'

(From a letter in *The Elizabethans*, edited by A. Nicoll; Cambridge 1957)

flourish in the severe court of Henry VII. The slim, male silhouette started to widen until it achieved the 'square box on two stalks' appearance of the familiar outline of Henry VIII.

The tunic or gown: This was a loose-fitting, full gown worn either long to the ground, or calf-length or knee-length according to the age of the wearer and the variations in the fashions of each particular time. It was rather like a huge, wide-collared, big-sleeved dressing gown. The sleeves could be long or short, and the garment could be simply a practical way of keeping warm or an opportunity for elaborate and costly decoration. Henry VIII might wear one of cloth of gold, encrusted with precious stones, lined and collared with fur, and braided with gorgeous colour. A country squire might wear a brown wool one with a darker brown collar. In contemporary illustrations they are worn hanging open to show the doublet or jerkin underneath, though in reality they must often have been crossed over and belted for warmth or convenience.

The doublet or jerkin: This was essentially a fitted jacket. It could be worn under the gown as a sort of tunic, open over the shirt like a waistcoat, or buttoned up to the low or high neck as a formal garment. It could have long sleeves, or be sleeveless to show the sleeves of a waistcoat or shirt. Detachable sleeves were sometimes laced on to the sleeveless version and showed the shirt through the gaps in the laces. Like the men's jackets of today, it could have the formality of a city business suit, or be the everyday wear of the labourer. It began as a low-necked garment which was worn open to the waist and showing the sleeves and front of an under tunic or shirt. It progressed, through various stages, to the stiff, high-necked doublet with the pointed front that we are familiar with from portraits of Elizabethan court. Though the countrified versions of this garment, or even a military-looking leather version, are straightforward enough to make, the formal court version is daunting, both practically and financially. The stiffened, padded, richly decorated fabric must be perfectly fitted to allow the actor to move, as well as to give the impression of rigidity in the body. An impression of this formality can be given by making a well fitting, high-necked waistcoat and finishing the armholes with epaulettes or rolls. An even simpler option is to use a version of the tabard worn over a shirt.

Cloaks: The circular cloak was worn in all lengths but has a particular place in late Tudor circles as a short indoor garment, worn over one shoulder, both shoulders, or under one arm and hanging down the back. It was flourished and tossed and used almost as a canvas of extra decoration and display on the backs and shoulders of the Tudor males. It is an equally effective device for the costumier. When Sir Walter Raleigh laid down his cloak in the mud to stop his queen getting her feet wet it was indeed a sacrifice, like making a pavement of Rolex watches to be trampled on today.

Breeches: It appears from contemporary paintings that breeches and hose were kept up by being tied with laces through eyelet holes in the waist of the doublet. The codpiece, a padded flap that covered the genitals and the join of the hose, was kept in place in the same way. Given the difficulty some men have of remembering to do up their fly buttons or zips, one cannot help suspecting that many of these points, as they were called, were left undone. However much of a daily challenge they were to the Tudor male, they are a decorative boon to the costume designer, and the neatness or otherwise of the way they are tied can be most expressive of character.

Breeches probably started life as underpants, but evolved into a much more complicated garment as tunics shortened and they came into more public view. Their varying shape – with or without codpiece, plain and close fitting, bulging like two footballs over the upper thighs, padded and ending just above the knee, striped with stiff ribbon of a different cloth, wide- or narrow-legged – is bewildering in its complication until you view the silhouette as a whole. Then it becomes clear that the shape of the breeches balances the figure created by the different doublets and headwear. The most manageable ones for simple Tudor costume are the knee-length 'venetians'. They will create the right impression on the audience though they are not actually correct as fashionable wear throughout the whole period. They have the advantage of dispelling many of the problems associated with codpieces, also wrinkled tights and the rather ridiculous look the more extreme fashions acquire when they are not absolutely convincing in every detail. However, the potential comedy of the codpiece should not be forgotten, and there are many Tudor jokes that lead one to believe it is not only a modern sense of humour that finds them funny.

Hose: At the time, 'hose' sometimes referred to the breeches as well as the tights or stockings that covered the nether parts not covered by doublet and breeches. They had a triangular

Useful ideas.

flap that could be untied so you could pee without taking your tights off; they were attached to the upper garments with ties or laces. The fastenings are useful punctuation for the designer, and can be neat and decorative, or very rough and ready according to the class of the wearer. Sometimes they were striped vertically, or the two legs were different colours. A decorative garter might be worn below the knee.

The shirt: A particularly useful garment if you are not dressing your actors in full costume. Shirts were full, low necked at the beginning of the era and high to the neck later, ending in a collar, small frill, band or ruff. If using a ruff, end the collar with a band and attach the ruff separately. The full shirt often showed through a pattern of little slits or larger slashes in the fabric of the doublet or tunic.

Work clothes
When dressing actors for a range of social classes it is useful to remember that it is not only rich fabrics that are out of the financial reach of ordinary people. The cutting and fitting, as well as the expensive accessories, meant that the clothes we see in portraits of court life might cost more than the lifetime's wages of an ordinary clerk, let alone a labourer. Breeches and tunic unchanged since medieval times would still have been seen in country field, perhaps with a loose-fitting doublet or jacket.

Bags, pouches, baskets, sticks, aprons, belts and tools point to their trades. The rise in social standing would have been marked by how closely a man's clothes imitated those of the fashionable court.

Accessories
Gloves, hats, ruffs, purses and pouches, jewellery, including earrings for men. Swords, worn as a part of normal formal dress, can present a problem but the dagger, an easier alternative and habitual accessory, can give the costumier an opportunity for decoration of belt and hilt.

Clothes for Children
Upper class and wealthy children, once they emerged from the tight swaddling of baby-hood, were dressed as little adults for formal occasions. One hopes they were allowed some playtime in less tightly structured clothing, or that any child with a bit of gumption would have undone some buttons or laces to climb trees or play energetically when the grown-ups weren't looking. The shirt and hose or breeches of the boy, or the undershift of the girl, would have been more comfortable and economical playclothes for fast-growing children. This more relaxed type of dress, with a sleeveless doublet for the boys and a fitted bodice and long skirt for a girl, would make a simple costume that could change with the choice of fabric and accessories, the most telling of which would be the ruff and hat (the same as adult male hats) for the boys. The girls wore their hair long and loose under a small bonnet or coif, or the same hats as women.

4 LINEN, LACE AND CIVIL WAR 1603–1660

THE LIFE OF THE TIME AND ITS CLOTHES

Queen Elizabeth I – bald, toothless, difficult and beloved – died, and after 60 hours or so of muddy galloping, the messenger arrived in Edinburgh to tell King James of Scotland he was also King James I of England. News, even news so momentous, travelled slowly, and it is easy to forget how little most people knew of what was going on in their world. The court and its customs and costume was as remote to the average worker as we are to a tiny village in the heart of the Amazon jungle. The court dress that is shown to us in the portraits of the sixteenth and seventeenth centuries shows complicated, much decorated and carefully constructed clothes that would have been quite beyond the budget and experience of most of the people of Britain. And if they had worn them, it would have been impossible to

have done any manual work without spoiling the strictly structured effect. How could you draw water from the well when your skirt stuck out so far from your waist, and or do the weeding when you couldn't bend for the stiffness of your doublet?

Elizabeth's was a hard act for James to follow. Both of them were extravagant, opinionated, and jealous of their power, but the people loved Elizabeth and they didn't love charmless James. Yet during his reign, which glitters in our sights so much less brightly than hers, many of the greatest cultural landmarks of our heritage were created. These included buildings, painting, poetry, music and plays and, perhaps most influential of all to the development of the language of the people for the next four hundred and more years, the Authorised Version of the Bible, which rolled its powerful and beautiful phrases round the ears of literate and illiterate alike.

James ruffled everyone. Catholic Guy Fawkes tried to blow him up. Protestants demanded changes in the Prayer Book. The Pilgrim Fathers sailed off to create a Puritan community in North America away from corrupting high church influences. The palaces were full of foreign art flavoured with Catholic imagery. Parliament wasn't as certain as James was – and later his son Charles – of their divine right to spend the country's money as they pleased. Extravagant masques performed at court to glorify the monarchy gobbled up money that many thought should have been used to fight England's wars. James' son and successor inherited, and increased, the unrest.

Charles I's accession to the throne initiated a dramatic change in the fashions of England, the catalyst his high church practice and his French wife, Henrietta Maria. She was Roman Catholic, pretty and fashion-conscious, and the sombre influence on texture and colour from the Spanish court was replaced by the more pastoral and softer tendencies of the French one; the most obvious of these was a loosening of the clothes of both men and women. The strict lines of structured fabric softened, and bore more relation to the natural shape of the body. It was as if the clothes worn in Elizabeth's court stayed more or less the same cut, but most of the padding and stiffening and underclothes that adapted the body shape were thrown away: the heavy linings and braid that impeded the natural flow of the fabric, the sharp edges, and the stiff decoration, were all discarded. Cloth needed to mould and drape, not to hold its shape against all odds.

This relationship with the continent, where French fashions, draperies and decoration were rioting in response to the influence of Baroque art, brought more lace and ribbons and extravagant fabrics to the stiff and subtle richness of the English court. A sober Puritan, dressed in grey wool with plain linen collar

> ... A sweet disorder in the dress
> Kindles in clothes a wantoness:
> A lawn about the shoulders thrown
> Into a fine distraction ...
> A careless shoestring, in whose tie
> I see a wild civility:
> Do more bewitch me than when art
> Is too precise in every part.
>
> Robert Herrick, 1591–1674. (A 'lawn' would have been a muslin scarf)

and cuffs, or even a quietly dressed parliamentarian, would have seen the display of Royalist colour and texture as a living embodiment of their king's high church and suspected popish sympathies.

Both James' and Charles' courts had been inward-looking, and the extravagant displays of performance and fashion were self-glorifying rites for the initiates – the courtiers and aristocracy; they were not for 'the people', who were supposed to be impressed enough by the fact that their king spoke with God's voice on earth. Consequently, although the influence of Inigo Jones' marvellous designs for royal performances must have led those who saw them to greater heights of extravagance and decoration in their dress, the farmer, even on high days and holidays, dressed in the long-lasting and practical garments he had always worn. To look at a portrait of Oliver Cromwell – confident, rough-cropped and powerful in buff leather – beside one of King Charles – reserved, refined but equally self-assured in his curls and lace – is to understand much of the heart of the rift that led to Civil War, and the scaffold for the king.

The court in the first half of the century was a closed affair. The fashionable display that went on within it could have had little influence on the outside world, and it is probable that the differences in Royalist and Puritan costume had been a feature of common dress long before the great division created by the Civil War took precedence. Many men and women must have worn clothes that hovered between the two. As a general rule, the clothes and accessories of the court circles were bedecked with flourishes and furbelows. The exclusive nature of James and his son Charles I would have kept these parading fashions to a very small circle, and more rural, though aristocratic, supporters of the royal family who lived out of court would have dressed in a style closer to our idea of a Puritan, with perhaps a flutter of lace at the collar or a showy hat decoration.

The deep falling collar, a strong sign to us of the Stuart years, replaced the ruff and stiffened collars, which have become such a significant accessory to Tudor fashion. This crisp division, as if one time switched off as another switched on, is, of course, quite inaccurate historically, but as few people in the audience will be costume historians, this clear difference in the silhouette is most useful to the costume designer. These deep collars edged with lace symbolize the Royalist cavaliers to us, and the plain white linen collar, the Puritan influence.

The difference in costume between the aristocratic and the middle classes, the Royalists and the Parliamentarians, the Roundheads and the Cavaliers, opens a window on an interesting and unusual view of the people of the time. The enclosed court, and the apparent lack of interest and affection of the first two Stuart rulers for their people, is reflected in their exclusive fashions. The quantity of extravagant decoration in the court clothes was seen only in those circles, and the middle classes do not appear to have imitated these extreme styles, even when dressed up in their very best to be recorded for posterity by the

Sober John Evelyn was robbed by two 'cutt-throats' on the highway of '… two rings, the one an emrald with diamonds, an onyx one engraved with his arm, and two boucles set with rubies and diamonds' as well as his sword and money.

portrait painter. The uncluttered silhouette they project appears to have more sympathy with the undecorated, modest dress of the Puritan. The buff jerkin – a simple, high-waisted jacket originally worn by soldiers and then adopted by many civilian men – seems to have had a strong influence on middle-class costume, and was, perhaps, worn by the Royalist more often than their portraits in frills and lace would lead us to believe. The dramatic opposition in costume at the time of the Civil War, when we imagine all who supported the king in plumed and ribbonned splendour, and all Cromwell's supporters in reserved and practical clothes, may not be as clear cut as it appears.

A beheaded king, no court, no more masques, no more extravagance, and stern Oliver Cromwell in charge: this was a heavy blow to the fashions of the first half of the century. The new austerity brought little change to the poor, however, many of whom harvested their crops, wove their cloth, smacked their children and patched their shoes oblivious of the shattering change to Britain's history. But it brought a huge change to the rich, and to anyone who knew what was going on, or had fought in the war, or whose families were split by their support of either Roundheads or Cavaliers. The difference between the costume of the upper and middle classes became less apparent as the delicate and opulent lace collars gave place to plain linen ones. Hats no longer waved with ostrich plumes, and knees and wrists lost rosettes and ribbons. Those with old-fashioned ideas clung to their lace and curls as comfort in those years of dull austerity, and the Puritans displayed their discrete dress as a badge of their faith. Steadfast Royalists, sporting their lace collars and silk sashes, rejoiced when Charles II, be-ribbonned, be-curled and fresh from the continent, paced stylishly back to London.

CREATING THE CLOTHES FOR THE STAGE

Clothes for Women

Heads and Headgear

Hair: Women's hair was worn long. It was flattish and smooth on top, and then divided into curled bunches at the sides. Short, curly fringes were worn, but the high hairline that had been the goal of every fashionable woman for a hundred or so years, had lost its hold on women.

Make-up: The use of make-up to enhance a fashionably delicate pallor was restricted to those of Royalist tendencies, as its frivolous connotations were at odds with puritanical ethics.

Royalist hats: Hats, when worn, were wide and plumed with feathers. More usual forms of head decoration were jewels, ribbons or feathers, woven or pinned into the hair.

Puritan hats: Typically a tall, untrimmed, wide-brimmed hat, rather like a witch's hat with the point chopped off flat; it would be tied under the chin, and sometimes put on over the close-fitting white linen cap worn by many Puritan and working women.

The veil: A piece of lightweight cloth covering the hair or drawn loosely at the back into a soft hood.

The cap: White or natural-coloured, close-fitting bonnets worn by Puritan or working women.

Feet and Footwear

Stockings hardly showed, and shoes, with rosettes for decoration on the fronts when appropriate, had medium heels.

Clothing the Body

Dresses: Women's dresses began to lose the almost masculine and square-shouldered rigidity of the Elizabethan era as the shoulder line dropped to reveal more of the neck and breast. The waistline of dresses rose, and the long, stiff, pointed panel at the front of the dress was shortened so it was less belly-stabbing. The fabric of the dresses softened, and lace and ribbons began to replace the stiff braid and heavy decoration. Bodices were still boned and the aristocratic female figure was still restrained, but the rigid structure and linings of the Elizabethan dresses were relaxed. Rich pastel and jewel-like colours came into fashion, and the skirt was full and gathered, sometimes with a train at the back. An over-skirt could be open at the front over the underskirt as a decorative device.

The sleeves were set low to give a sloping shoulder line; the considerable fullness was gathered into the armhole and again above or below the elbow, and edged with lace and garnished with ribbon. Collars and sleeves were trimmed with lace when women could afford it, unless they had puritanical tendencies, when the collar would be of plain linen and the plain long sleeves finished with a neat cuff. The gently glimmering satin colours of the court circle, set off by the white and cream lace and muslin of collars and frills, were worlds away from the bright glittering pageantry of the Tudor court 30 years before.

Those who disapproved of the lavish display of the king and his courtiers adopted sober

Seventeenth-century women.

colours and a simplified and modest style of dress in quiet shades of woollen cloth. Lace trimmings on dresses were abjured by Puritans and became almost the badge of a Royalist.

The gathered dresses of this era are complicated to cut and fit, and expensive to make. It may be found necessary to use a basic dress with a long gathered skirt, or a tight-fitting, low-necked leotard or body worn with a full, long skirt, and to make it appear to belong to the period with appropriate accessories. The distinguishing signs that have a most telling effect on the audience perception of character are the differences that point the Royalist or Puritan allegiance of the woman. The low necklines and sleeves trimmed with lace, the clusters of ribbons decorating shoulders or bodice, and the gleaming and beautiful colour of the fabric say 'Royalist' and 'rich', as surely as the plain linen collars and caps, high necks and lack of decoration say 'Puritan'.

The triangular scarf or round-edge scarf: A simple triangle of muslin, edged with lace, or plain, depending on the inclination of the wearer. It was worn round the neck like a separate collar and could be tucked into the front of the bodice or left to hang loose. A plain bodice and full skirt with one of these triangular scarves and other accessories and an appropriate hairstyle will do quite a good job of suggesting the time. The ends of the scarf can be brought together to a point in front and will give an impression of a pointed bodice where none exists.

Cloaks: Cloaks with loose, floppy hoods were worn as protection from the cold by both working women and gentry.

Working Clothes
Apart from the very poor who covered themselves in whatever they could afford, working

> Humble wedding finery for a working couple: 'Upon Tuesday my Love and I went to market not far distant where we did provide ourselves of apparel both linen and wool'. (*The Courtship Narrative* of Leonard Wheatcroft, Derbyshire Yeoman; The Whiteknights Press, Reading)

women wore clothes that followed much the same principles as the rich Puritan women. Small, white linen caps kept the hair off the face. A white triangular scarf worn modestly round the shoulders and an apron were worn over a simple bodice and ankle-length skirt. These skirts, as in other eras when working women wore long skirts, would have been tucked up to reveal the petticoat when it was necessary to keep it out of the muck at ground level.

Accessories
Hair decorations, gloves, muffs.

Clothes for Men
Heads and Headgear
Hair: Hair was worn longer and longer as the century progressed. By the time the civil war began, the curling locks had become a badge of support for the king, and the shorter-cropped hair was the mark of Cromwellian allegiance. Small moustaches and neat-trimmed pointed beards were worn by the king, so presumably also by those who followed court fashion.

The tall hat: A tall, small-brimmed hat, rather like a chopped-off witch's hat, developed from the tall Elizabethan hat. This started as a general fashion, but then became a hat particular to Puritan dress. Although these can be made from scratch, another, and

Seventeenth-century men.

perhaps easier option is to buy a version from a fancy-dress shop. These are rarely solid enough to look convincing, but they can be made more substantial with a covering of felt.

The broad-brimmed hat: A wide-brimmed, rounded, crowned felt hat whose brim could be rolled up on one side and fastened to the crown. The decoration of these hats – either with plumes of feathers for the dashing Royalist, a plain dark hatband for the strictly puritanical, or the many degrees between the two – will show the style of the man.

Feet and Footwear

Men wore boots much of the time, a custom which for the costumier is a knife to the heart of the budget. At first, these were fairly close-fitting with round toes, then they developed wide tops, rather like a bucket, and square toes. The saving grace for the strapped-for-cash costumier is the broad and often decorated fastening band over the instep; this makes it possible to disguise the join if you have had to add a boot top to a shoe.

Shoes were often fastened over the long tongue, which then flapped over the fastening; this is another saving grace, as a false tongue can be added which will disguise, to a certain extent, a modern leather shoe.

Clothing the Body

The doublet or jacket: The waist of the front-buttoned doublet rose gradually and became less rigid. The short, stiffened band that jutted out from the waist lengthened, flopped and sometimes divided until the doublet became a rather high-waisted jacket that covered the hips with a slightly pointed front. A further development in fashion was to leave the doublet unbuttoned from just below the chest to show the shirt beneath. This shirt showed again through the doublet sleeves, which were slashed with one or more vertical lines. At the very end of the period it showed in a new place, when the fashionable doublet only just reached the waist and the shirt puffed out between jacket and breeches. A simplified and undecorated version of the longer doublet or jerkin, with its row of buttons down the front, became the standard garment for Puritans, most ordinary people and soldiers.

The features of this jacket which distinguish it particularly as belonging to the period are the collar and cuffs. During the Civil War, and in the years before and after it, men and their families demonstrated their political allegiance through the decoration of their clothes; the signs they used to do this are as clear to today's audience as they were to the people of the time. Thus the collar worn by the Royalists was white and large, and seems designed to give the wearer an opportunity to demonstrate his wealth by its trimmings. Lace was expensive, noticeable and often rare, and the ability to judge the quality of lace must have been a manly and refined accomplishment, as is the ability to recognize a fine wine today. The shape of the edge of white lace on a darker cloth beneath shows as well on-stage today as it did in the past at court, and an extravagant lace cuff sitting against the dark or coloured sleeve of the jacket gives an unmistakable message of richness and refinement to the onlooker.

The other extreme – the plain, deep, white or natural-coloured linen collar and cuff, strict in form and devoid of decoration – seems to defy the complication of lace with its firm, straightforward lines. Details such as the slashing to show the shirt sleeves, the braiding of the hems, and the clusters of ribbons and gorgeous sash which mark the Royalist, are challenged by the opposition of the clean lines, perhaps decorated with a line of plain buttons and a buckle or two, of the Puritan.

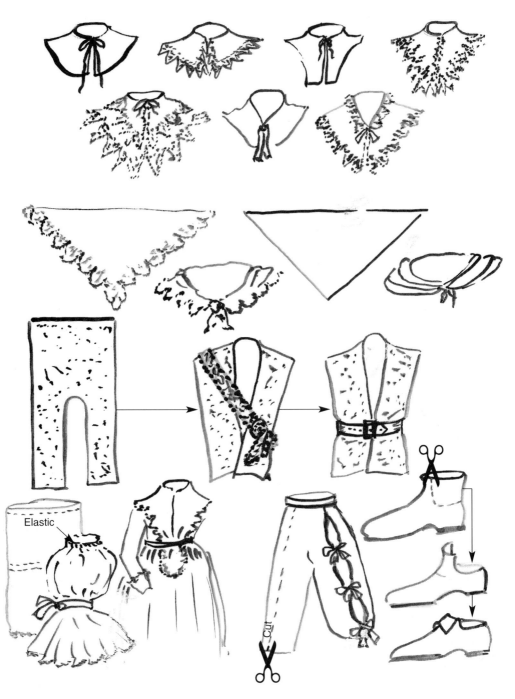

Useful ideas.

Breeches. The breeches that were worn with this doublet reached to just below the knee, and it was usual for the cloth and colour of the two to match. They also matched the style of the doublet, as the knee-band provided a point for more frills, ruffles and ribbons, or for a stern and business-like buckle. Breeches could be full and gathered into a band, straight and loose below the knee, or narrowed over the thigh and fitting closely at the knee.

The shirt. The shirt was full, and it is the collar and cuffs that are the distinguishing mark of the period. The wide, flopping collar sat over the neck of the jacket, and the cuffs were turned back over jacket sleeves, or were invisible under it. A more fashion-conscious male might wear the loose lace cuffs of his shirt falling over his hands. The shirt has an added importance at this time, as its fullness could puff out through slashes in the sleeves or body of the doublet or between the doublet and breeches.

The cloak. Cloaks, hip- thigh- or ground-length, hung in soft folds, and had unstiffened, wide, turnover collars.

The sash or cross-belt. The sash could be worn over one shoulder, usually the right, as this produced the natural slant for a man drawing a sword. The cross-belt could be a strictly practical band that supported the sword, an opportunity for a decorative transverse band across the body, or a combination of the two.

A description of a country clothes lent as a disguise: '... a leather doublet full of holes and half black with grease above the sleeves, collar and waist ... the hose were grey, much darned and clouted (mended) especially about the knees, under which he had a pair of flannel riding stockings ... with the tops cut off'. (*Life Cycles in England, 1560–1720*. (Mary Abbott, published 1996 by Routledge)

Work Clothes
Full shirt and loose-fitting breeches, woollen stockings and shoes form a base, and would vary in quality according to the status of the man. Waistcoats, either thigh length or short, would echo the shape of the doublets and jackets, and aprons, cloaks and belts add definition to the outline.

Accessories
Hats, swords, gloves, sashes, restrained jewellery, mostly rings.

Clothes for Children

Children were dressed in the same way as the adults of the class to which they belonged. The frills of the Royalist and the plainer dress of the parliamentarian applied to the children, as to their parents. Little girls of all classes are sometimes pictured in their ankle-length skirts wearing close-fitting little linen bonnets tied under the chin over their loose hair. Royalist boys and all girls wore their hair long and curled, but Puritan boys' hair was cut.

5 CULTURE, CURLS AND THE COUNTRY HOUSE 1660–1789

THE LIFE OF THE TIME AND ITS CLOTHES

In 1660, Charles II became king, following a period when England was without monarch and court, and the frivolities and artistic pleasures of life had been suppressed. The elaborate Baroque style that had been influencing every form of art in Europe, had been kept at bay by the puritanical influence of Oliver Cromwell and his supporters. As Charles and his entourage entered London and processed through the decorated streets and cheering crowds, the influence of Versailles and other European centres of culture followed in his wake. So did their dress, for both men and women: lace, fur, brocade, ruffles, ribbons, buttons and bows

High fashion returns to England: '... all the silk waistcoats with silver and gold edgings, were eclipsed in an instant. I have been told he had on a cut velvet coat of cinnamon colour, lined with pink satten, embroidered all over with gold; his waistcoat, which was cloth of silver, was embroidered with gold likewise ... it was all in the French fashion ...' (*The Adventures of Joseph Andrews* by Henry Fielding, published J. M. Dent & Sons)

and long curls gleamed in the cultured court. Many of these lords and commoners who cheered in the streets at that glorious procession were to die a few years later when the plague, and the cleansing but terrible

Great Fire of London rampaged through the city.

It was an era of cultural change in Britain. Charles II headed a court that took its arts seriously, and despite a hiccup after his death in 1688 when his brother became king until ousted by popular and Protestant demand, the refinement of the culture of Britain was to continue throughout the eighteenth century.

As so often happens, the architects led the way. The buildings of the time have remained with us as a benchmark of pro-portion, grace and humanity: Hawksmoor's churches, solemn and glorious; the gracious sweep of the royal crescent in Bath; the Palladian villas, their calm formal gardens laid out with mathematical precision – these were a contemporary response to classical ideals, and as such a real innovation. They provided a setting for the men and women whose education led them to an enlightened and spiritual view of their world, and a robust attitude to more worldly pleasure.

The clothes of both men and women were heavily decorated, and the portraits of the time show us that a stylized deportment must have been an essential lesson in the education of the fashionable courtier. The full-skirted coats and elaborate wigs of the men, and the yards of expensive cloth that made the complicated dresses of the women, had to be carefully manipulated by their wearers. It would have taken hours of practice to manage all those canes, muffs, handkerchiefs, fans, swords and gloves with the apparently unstudied ease required by a person of distinction. Extremes of decoration and frippery apparent in their clothes may seem at loggerheads with the spirit of serious study of religion, arts and landscape pursued by the upper classes of the time; but the baroque God, all-powerful but not puritanical, looked down relatively tolerantly at the royal adulterers from his painted gilt-framed blue heaven in church and drawing room.

Trade flourished and brought with it new ideas, fabrics and raw cotton from the colonies to excite the inventors of fashion. By the end of the period the invention of the flying shuttle, the 'Spinning Jenny', and the new spinning and knitting machines, had revolutionized the industry and could do the work in a fraction of the time it had taken men, women and children to do it by hand. Other countries demanded the fashionable and economical cloth created in the British factories. And another profitable import and desirable acces-sory for the wealthy and fashionable woman was also traded along with the cotton crop: the little page boy, his black skin and exotic costume providing a dramatic contrast to the powdered whiteness and gleaming satin of his mistress.

The curling, ruffled and almost feminine profusion that decorated the men at the beginning of the period steadied to a sober and restrained silhouette by its end. As the eighteenth century progressed, a strange reversal occurred in male and female fashion. As the men's coats became narrower and less flamboyant, the women widened their skirts and added more flounces; the men's cravats became higher and lost their lace; the women lowered their necklines and drew attention to their breasts.

The availability of cotton brought a lightness and prettiness to the ladies' dresses, and began to replace the heavy brocades and satins in the latter half of the century. The

> ... a fashionable lady who '... has screwed her body into so fine a form (as she calls it) that she dares no more stir a hand, lift up an arm, or turn her head aside ...' (*The Lady's Looking Glass* by Aphra Behn, published by Routledge)

waistline settled where nature had put it. Though the bodices were heavily boned, at least the stays ended at the waist, and hips and bosom could expand at will. Intelligent women, even though their marriage might be arranged by their fathers for political or financial gain, had a voice of their own, and could engage in the witty or discursive conversations that were one of the chief pleasures of the leisured classes. Men could be trading abroad for long periods, and often succumbed to the diseases so rife in the colonies or at sea, and some of their wives were sufficiently educated and emancipated to continue the family business alone. There is a feeling of definite, though grudging, respect for these lively women, which is evident in the literature of the time.

Wealthy young gentlemen completed their education with a continental tour, and the influence of the sights and paintings they experienced on this journey could be seen in their clothes as well as in the great houses and gardens they built on their return. They commissioned portraits that show them gazing calmly from these houses over their acres of rolling countryside. As the century progressed, their full-skirted coats narrowed, decoration was restrained, and the forerunner of the three-piece suit arrived when coat, waistcoat and breeches were made of the same cloth. Their clothes might seem to us heavily ornamented, but to their counterparts in Europe they were a model of simplicity and good taste. Thus men and women of discernment across the channel wore clothes 'à l'anglaise'.

The middle classes gained in financial and social stability, prospering with the increased opportunities in trade as Britain gained more power overseas. Despite political and religious problems, the complications of accession of various monarchs, and the wars and internal struggles, it is clear from the literature, archi-

tecture and paintings which are their legacy that the middle and upper classes were creative, inventive and morally aware. Many made fortunes and were able to accrue dowries to tempt impoverished aristocrats to marry their daughters. The agricultural work that had always been a staple source of employment in the countryside was supplemented by the need to provide exportable goods to load the hundreds of ships sailing off to trade abroad. This gave employment to many of the lower classes.

Life was hard for the unlucky or indigent. Those who didn't manage to earn an honest penny were punished with terrifying severity, and their dependants left to struggle on by themselves. No foreign tours for the poor unless they were convicts sentenced to transportation and a dangerous journey to the colonies. Many sank in the harsh, dank underworld of the towns or the mud of the countryside, drank themselves to death, were hung for petty crimes, or starved in prison.

As always, it must be remembered that in portraits, men and women are very often dressed in their most spectacular finery. The trade in wool and cotton that was so buoyant at the time must have been supported by the middle and upper classes, and the success of this economy must have relied on the fact that they, the people who spent money on cloth, would buy the product. Flipping through a collection of contemporary pictures, the impression of silk, satin, velvet, brocade and embroidery is strong. But many of these ladies in their huge skirted dresses that used up so many yards of cloth, must have been dressed in cotton, and its lighter and more pastoral effect would lead naturally to the simple dresses and shepherdess hats of the end of the period. Men's coats and breeches would have been made in the wool broadcloth for which England was famous, more often than they would have shimmered in satin.

It is probable that the new exposure of women's forearms, together with the complicated etiquette that surrounded the use of the fan, which displayed the arms and wrists, caused the same sort of stir in society as the exposure of the thigh by the mini-skirt of the 1960s.

Gradually, towards the end of the period, a new simplicity in women's dress took hold. The elegance of the men, and the lighter, more natural clothes of the women, create a balanced effect that seems to reflect the intellectual parity which is apparent in much of the writing of the time.

CREATING THE CLOTHES FOR THE STAGE

Clothes for Women

Heads and Headgear

Hair: Hair was powdered on formal occasions, and often dressed with elaborate care and decoration. Women's curls and the wide outline of the end of the seventeenth century were replaced by a small neat head that, at the end of the period, was once again enlarged both in height and width by elaborately dressed hair.

Make-up: It was fashionable and acceptable in many circles for women to wear make-up, and false beauty spots – known as patches – directed attention to beautiful features, or detracted from less lovely ones.

Caps: Lace or muslin caps were worn from the last decades of the seventeenth century throughout the period, but they took very different shapes. The fashion for wearing a high, wired, fan-shaped peak at the front of the cap, which could add considerably to the height of the wearer, was replaced by a little frilled cap, sometimes decorated with ribbons, which could be worn under the hat as well as

on its own. These caps had wide or narrow strings of the same cloth, which could be pinned into the hair, tied under the chin, or left to fall in apparently casual disarray. Towards the end of the period, when women's heads were dressed large and high, a loose, light hood sometimes covered the hair. The illustrations of the time show us a wonderful variety of these gauzy caps that can be used when a wig cannot be afforded.

The tricorn: This hat was worn by women, sometimes in miniature form at the end of the seventeenth century, and can be made by attaching the brim of a felt hat to the crown in three equally spaced places.

Hats: These came into vogue again as hairstyles became more complex after the middle of the eighteenth century. They were often both wide and high, and would be decorated with feathers, flounces and frills, thus further enlarging their silhouette. A straw hat, with more restrained trimming, accompanied the simplified dresses of the women at the end of the period. The exaggerated shape of the hats can be recreated on the base of a modern fine straw or felt hat.

Legs and Feet

Stockings hardly showed, but could be white or coloured. The buckles, ribbons, rosettes and other decoration that adorned the front of the small-heeled shoes make the female footwear of the time easy to reproduce by adapting modern shoes.

Clothing the Body

Bodices, skirts and dresses: women matched men in the exuberant decoration of their clothes – but unlike the men, they continued to deck their clothes with ruffled ribbon, lace and embroidery throughout the period until overcome by the vogue for an urban version of

Restoration and Georgian women.

rustic simplicity. The slim-waisted gown over the careful boning of the stays emphasized the rounded bust, and controlled the lines of the upper body. The decoration of the bodice emphasized, by its triangular shape, the smallness of the waist and the curves of the bosom. The full, long sleeves, often arranged in a series of puffs, shrank and shortened into an elbow-length, fairly close-fitting sleeve ending at the elbow and decorated with frills and lace ruffling over the forearm. In order to show these cuffs to advantage, the elbows were held out from the body and this, in turn, emphasized the smallness of the waist.

The skirts were worn over petticoats that were stiffened at the beginning of the century, and then, swelled by hoops and padding, held out the fullness of the skirt like a cloth over a lampshade, in whatever shape and dimensions fashion decreed at the time. The overskirt could be open at the front and pulled back and up over the underskirt. The arrangement of the draperies and the decoration of the edges of the fronts were an opportunity for imaginative and complicated decoration.

It is difficult to suggest the complicated dress of the time in a simple manner. A double-layered skirt, with the top one looped up on the hips, a tight, low-necked top and a black band round the neck with a flower or rosette at the side can, with suitable hair, accessories and deportment, create the right outline.

Scarves and cloaks: The hooped petticoat made cloaks and scarves or wraps the most practical way of keeping warm. Cloaks were sometimes hooded and could be long or hip length. The scarf could be worn round the neck and tucked into or tied over the bodice to protect the breast, in its revealing low-cut bodice, from the weather or prying eyes. A large triangle was sometimes crossed across the chest and tied at the back with its ends hanging down over the skirt of the gown.

The apron: Aprons were, of course, worn for practical purposes to protect clothes from dirt. But they were also adopted as a fashion accessory, and the little muslin, silk, lace or embroidered apron was a pretty addition to many fashionable toilettes.

Work Clothes
The ability to follow fashion depended entirely on income, and working people did the best they could to follow fashion or keep warm and decent. Colour and texture is a useful way of distinguishing status at this time: the poorer the woman, the coarser and duller the cloth. Working women wore plain versions of the tight-bodiced, full-skirted dresses of the gentry, often with a scarf or *fichu* tucked in at the neck. The fashion of tucking up the overskirt so that the petticoat showed in front was common, as was the wearing of aprons and caps.

Accessories
Muffs, fans, small decorative bags, gloves, rosettes on ribbon at neck and wrist, canes, jewellery in the hair as well as ear rings, necklaces and brooches, and pretty well anything that could be carried in such a way as to display forearms, wrists and hands.

Clothes for Men
Heads and Headgear
Hair: Men, clean-shaven except perhaps for the narrowest little moustache, wore wigs of luxuriant curls over their shaved heads. This

> Moll disguises herself as a maid in '... an ordinary stuff-gown, a blue apron and a straw hat,' and again '... as a servant-maid in a round cap and straw hat'. (*Moll Flanders* by Daniel Defoe, published by Wordsworth Editions)

Restoration and Georgian men.

curly adornment could be tied in a tail, or put in a black silk bag at the back to stop it getting in the way of lively action. Men's wigs, whether full and curling onto the shoulders or drawn back in a queue behind, can present a financial problem to the costumier. It is better to comb the hair back and attach a false tail of hair with a simple wide black bow than to use a badly fitting wig. It may not be correct, but it will not attract the audience's attention as much as would an ill-made wig.

Make-up: Make-up was used occasionally, but not invariably, by the fashionable men of the time. Young men who dressed in the height of fashion; and older ones who wished to disguise the ravages of time or disease, powdered and patched as they looked at their reflections in the looking glass. This period is one of the few eras in which men have openly made up their faces.

The tricorne: A round hat with its wide brim turned up on three sides to create the triangular hat we associate with highwaymen and town criers; it was sometimes decorated with braid. This is a particularly strong sign to an audience of the late seventeenth and early eighteenth century. It can be created from a modern, wide-brimmed felt hat by turning up the brim in three places. It can be afforded when a wig is out of the question.

The smoking cap: A close-fitting, often embroidered and tasselled brimless cap, or a turban-shaped soft hat used informally indoors when the wig was not worn.

The round hat: A wide-brimmed, crowned hat. This was worn rather flat and much feathered at the end of the seventeenth century; in its unfeathered state, it then became the property of the less fashionable.

It was the men in their breeches who had the expensive problem of showing a neatly stockinged leg: the female leg was hidden under the skirt. 'For a poor man going among strangers, I have found useful things to be silk thread and pins the same colour as one's clothes (silk thread, that is, of the kind used for knitting stockings)'. (From *Samuel Johnson's Diary*, published by Oxford University Press)

Legs and Feet
Stockings were usually white with formal dress, but could be patterned or coloured for normal day wear. Shoes were usually black, and the bow or buckled strap and big tongue of the early years evolved into a less elaborate style with a buckle at the front. The high, and often red-painted heel of the late seventeenth century had descended into a low-heeled pump by the end of the eighteenth.

Clothing the Body
The coat. The equivalent of a suit jacket nowadays was a knee-length, waisted coat with splits or vents at the side and the back. The coat started straight-fronted and wide skirted, and progressed later in the century to having a curved front and narrower style. The cuffs on the long sleeves, the pocket flaps, and the buttons and buttonholes were distinctive and decorative features of its design. These coats

Pepys buys new clothes for job interviews: '...a velvet cloak, two new cloth suits, black plain both; a new shag gown, trimmed with gold buttons and twist; with a new silk hat and silk tops for my legs, and many other things. And also two periwigs.' (*Pepys Diary* published by Bell and Hyman Ltd)

and their accompanying waistcoats and breeches were often made in elaborate and costly cloth, and richly embroidered and braided.

The frock (coat): This began as a less formal affair than the coat, with a looser fit and a turn-over collar. The buttons and pocket flaps still punctuated its outline, but we can imagine the wearer settling to a comfortable breakfast when wearing it, rather than sitting poised and nibbling on the edge of the chair. The frock followed the variations dictated by fashion in a less extreme and more comfortable manner than the more formal coat.

The waistcoat: The waistcoat, particularly in this period, is most useful to the costume designer creating for a small budget. In historical reality it would have been most unlikely that a gentleman would be seen on any public occasion in his shirtsleeves. However, for theatrical purposes the coat, which is so expensive and difficult to make, can be dispensed with, along with the wig – also expensive and difficult to make – and the actor can appear in shirt, cravat, waistcoat and breeches. However, this will only give an impression of a gentleman of the time if the shirt is white, and the same rules of dress apply to all characters.

The waistcoat, a little shorter than the coat at first, and cut off at the waist by the end of the century, followed the fashion of the coat. It could be full skirted, braided and embroidered, or a simple woollen cloth garment to wear when digging the garden. It echoed the coat's punctuation of buttons, buttonholes and pocket flaps.

Breeches: Breeches were worn, not trousers. They ended below the knee, and although baggy at first, fitted the upper class leg more and more closely as the eighteenth century

progressed. The workers, and those not so keen to show an elegant leg to the ladies, wore a baggier affair that gave more room for active movement. The fabric of coat, waistcoat and trousers was often the same, as is the three-piece suit of the businessman today.

Shirts and cravats: Shirts were full in both body and sleeves, with frills at the cuffs. They were worn with a cravat at first, and then with a stock. Whether frilled or plain, twisted or lacy, elaborate or simple, the line of the neckwear was high and usually white. This neckwear and also the wide shirtsleeves, perhaps worn with a long sleeveless waistcoat, are another useful indication of period when the expense of a coat is too much for the budget. Cravats and stocks can be tied from a straight strip of cloth of a suitable length to recreate the various fashions of the time. With a complicated cravat, it is often more successful with some actors if it is created in the wardrobe and its frills and folds then stitched into shape: it is then put on ready made and fastened at the back.

Cloaks: By this time cloaks had become an outdoor garment worn for warmth and protection from the weather. They often had turnover, or wide cape-like collars.

Sashes: The sash was a wide and sometimes fabulously decorated length of cloth wound round the waist over the coat with the ends hanging down at the side.

Work Clothes
The frock, that useful coat, loose-fitting and big-pocketed, can be seen in a simplified and clumsier cut on working men, when it is often worn with a round hat rather than a tricorn. The linen smock, loose and knee length, was worn by agricultural workers, as was the long waistcoat over shirt and breeches.

Useful ideas.

Accessories
Gloves, walking canes with tasselled decoration, sashes and decorative baldrics, beautiful swords for decorative rather than warlike purpose, handkerchiefs trimmed with lace, snuffboxes.

Clothes for Children

Once children had grown out of being swaddled little bundles, they were dressed as small versions of their parents, though very little boys were still dressed as girls, probably until they could be relied on not to wet their breeches.

Most portraits reflect upper-class children in formal and restrictive dress. They must have had less expensive clothes for everyday wear unless their parents were rich enough not to worry about the destruction of the silks and satins. Surely they must have chucked off their elaborate outer clothes to play, and simplicity must have reigned more commonly than appears.

The indigent may be clothed from the trimmings of the vain ...! ... The next day I had the satisfaction of finding my daughters employed in cutting up their trains into Sunday waistcoats for Dick and Bill. (*The Vicar of Wakefield*)

6 JANE AUSTEN AT HOME AND REBELLION ABROAD 1789–1840

THE LIFE OF THE TIME AND ITS CLOTHES

The revolution of 1789 may have happened in France, but it reverberated through fashionable, as well as political Britain. France was too busy with the aftermath of its turmoil to lead fashion as it had, but those aristocrats who escaped the guillotine by fleeing across the Channel brought a different interest in clothes to the upper classes. Rebellion was in British, as well as French, air.

All was not easy in the mills of Britain, though their cloth was of excellent quality. The new inventions in spinning and weaving meant that many people stopped working in their own safe cottages and went to» work in factories. Men, women and very young children laboured long hours, often in horrific and dangerous conditions, and a huge chasm gaped between the rich, who owned the factories, and the poor, who worked in them. The products of this powerful and expensive machinery paid for the careful upbringing of the owner's children, and this was itself an investment that could enable those children to cross another gaping chasm, that between the middle and the upper classes. The newly harnessed power of steam, added to the power of the waterwheel, put so many men out of work that it must have seemed a devilish, rather than a wonderful, power to those hungry families. Rebellion burst out in places when men were desperate enough to smash the new machines and defy the new law that forbade the forming of what would now be called trade unions.

More of the population had access to

rudimentary education, and by the end of this period a large proportion of the working class could read and find out more about how others lived. It was easier to travel and to move goods about the country. Canals and waterways, roads, bridges and the first railways meant that the middle and upper classes, who were not chained to mines, sweatshops and the soil, could move about the country with greater freedom. And when they weren't moving about the country admiring its beauty, drawing its landscapes and reciting poetry on its moors, they were reading – avidly and excitedly reading.

There were libraries, and the novel was as great a diversion as television is to us. Fashion was affected by the passionate life that was portrayed in the stories and poetry of the time, and in the thrilling victory of the Duke of Wellington (in his famous boots!) at the Battle of Waterloo. Though Britain was moving towards a new industrial age, the literature, painting and architecture fuelled a pull towards a romantic past. The most obvious and dramatic effect on clothes of this revival of interest in the classical world was the gradual rise of the position of the female waist to just below the armpits, and the freeing of the body from the corseted restraint of the previous years. It would have been the most extraordinary day for women when they emerged from their bedrooms and went downstairs in what must have felt like a near naked display of muslin and cotton print.

This style, this classical revival, had its origins in the Mediterranean sunshine, and women and girls shivered in the grey damp of an English February. So there came into fashion the many means of keeping out the damp chill: a short jacket called a spencer, overtunics, shawls, cloaks, muffs and the overcoat or cloak that could give extra protection to shoulders with its wide-layered collar.

Of course, this didn't happen immediately. The waist rose gradually. Skirts slowly became less voluminous. Muslin scarves covered the upper chest, and ringlets and bonnets prevailed. The older generation must have been shocked by the uncorseted, light petticoated display of the female form, and continued to wear the old fashions from choice, as poor people had to do from economy. Indeed, this armpit-high waist was not flattering to any female who had lost her high-breasted youth, and corsets were still used by those who were unlucky enough to have an inappropriate shape and fashion-conscious enough to care. Women lost their elaborate hairstyles and complicated wigs, and it was not unusual to see a young lady with a head of short curls. Thus society became accustomed to the new, natural shape, and women were free to enjoy the pleasure of moving their limbs and bending at the waist for the first time since the Tudors began power-dressing in the sixteenth century.

Men's clothes echoed this simplicity. Embroidery, frills and powdered wigs were discarded and replaced by a simplified costume. British tailoring was much admired and frequently copied abroad, as was the smooth woollen cloth woven in its mills. A square-cut, short waistcoat under a simple, narrow coat was a style adopted first by the fashion-conscious and gradually throughout society,

'She tells me that we owe her master for the silk dyeing. My poor old muslin has never been dyed yet. It has been promised to be done several times.' Jane Austen asks her sister to buy her seven and a half yards of '... a plain brown cambric muslin for morning wear' to add to the pink and yellow ones in her wardrobe. (Letter from Jane Austen to her sister, published by Penguin Classics)

The Regency sports car! A young man shows off to a girl that '... his equipage was altogether the most complete of its kind in England, his carriage the neatest, his horse the best goer, and himself the best coachman'. (*Northanger Abbey* by Jane Austen, published Penguin Classics)

though the powdered wigs were retained for use by footmen and liveried servants, and extraordinarily enough, are still in use today on formal, royal and some legal occasions. Trousers fitted the thigh and lower leg closely, though they had enough fullness in the seat for the gentleman to ride with ease – a fast horse or a natty carriage was the equivalent of a sports car today!

Children's little bodies were freed from heavy skirts and unkind stays. The lucky ones ran about with easy freedom in the light dresses, short jackets and loose-fitting trousers. The rest, despite the laws that limited the length of a child's working day, laboured to supplement their parent's income and keep the family from the miserable workhouse. Other boys and girls, who today might be still at junior school, went into service in the country houses where, though the work was unrelenting, they were at least assured food and clothing.

These country houses were one of the signposts on the road to success, and proof that it was now possible to achieve status through earned wealth as well as through a well-rooted family tree. Any novel or biography relating to the time shows us the importance of this little world, this badge of gentility to which most young gentlemen and all young and marriageable ladies aspired. The fashionable architect and garden designer employed by the owner to create these houses and their surrounding

parks were replaced, when their work was finished, by the huge number of people required to run these estates. Maids and grooms, cooks and scullery maids, gardeners and footmen, nurses and governesses were engaged and dressed in liveries and uniforms and aprons to reflect the taste and wealth of the owner.

But a rebellious sea existed between the fantastic sugar cake of the Prince Regent's Pavilion in Brighton, the elegant country houses, their rolling green parks planted with a confidence that future generations of their families would see the maturity of the young trees, and the sordid slum dwellings and workhouses of the poor. Parliament tried to pour oil on these simmering waters by demonstrating that the aristocratic and paternalistic social system could work for the benefit of the working class. Victoria became queen at a time when reforming forces were rallying to close that gap.

CREATING THE CLOTHES FOR THE STAGE

Clothes for Women
Heads and Headgear
Hair: Girls wanted curls throughout this period, so get to work with the curling tongs! It is of great advantage to the costumier that the curly head of short hair was seen in fashionable circles, and the difficulties of using hairpieces and wigs can be avoided. When hair was long, it was worn up, often bound with ribbons or decorated with ornaments or feathers, and the ends curled into ringlets.

Hats: It is certain from the great variation of hats in this time that bonnets were of great interest to them, and the literature of the time tells us that bonnet trimming was a happy accomplishment of most young ladies and working women.

Women of the early nineteenth century.

Bonnets: The shape varied from big-brimmed, high-crowned and feathered, through to the neat little bonnets on which the brim and crown formed a continuous, almost horizontal line. Some had a soft crown and a stiff brim. Bonnets of all styles and shapes appropriate for the fashions of the time can be created by cutting, stitching and reshaping straw or felt modern hats.

The easiest way to make a base on which to create a design is to remove the back third of the brim from a modern hat and use ribbons tied under the chin to shape the remaining portion of the brim into a bonnet. The way the hats are trimmed provides the message for the audience regarding the character and status of the woman. The trimming of bonnets in illustrations of the time may look, at first glance, frighteningly complicated; however, when you look more carefully you will see that the component parts are easy to recreate from a combination of a re-cut modern hat with ruffles, ribbons, flowers and feathers.

Caps: Older women wore muslin, cotton or lace caps indoors and outdoors under their bonnets. They could be high, covered with lace and very elaborate, or just neat little mob-caps with a few ruffles at the front and sides. In the latter years of the period they became fashionable for young women, and delicate lace and net versions were concocted to accompany evening dress. Servants and working women wore caps throughout the period. The choice of fabric for a cap, particularly a frilly, high-standing or elaborately pleated one, will make a considerable difference to its effect onstage. If made in a cloth that creases easily it may look good on the first night, but unless it is laundered and ironed with lengthy attention, it will lose its freshness and delicacy after the first wash. Give the cloth a crumple-inducing squeeze before you use it and make sure it springs back when you release it. The audience will not know you are using an authentic fabric – they will just see a creased wreck.

Turbans: Evening turbans were worn, and often displayed an exotic influence in their cloth as well as their shape. They can prove a useful device for quick changes when there is no time to create an elaborate evening hair-style. They cover the hair and with, perhaps, a few false curls can create an alteration of style in a few seconds. Turbans can be formed on the crown section of a cut-down felt hat, and decorated with padded rolls, feathers and brooches.

Legs and Feet
White or cream opaque stockings were worn. The fashionable foot was small, light and narrow. Low-heeled light pumps, a cross between a ballet shoe and a court shoe, can be painted or dyed to match a dress. Short, lightweight ankle boots could be worn with outdoor costume.

Clothing the Body
Dresses: The combination of the position of the waist, the relative size of the hair-style or bonnet shape, and the fullness of the skirt, are

Regarding the eccentric: '... These two ladies looked just like two old men. They always dressed in dark cloth (riding) habits with short (ankle-length) skirts, high shirt collars, white cravats and men's hats, with their hair cut short'. ... And the fashionable '... in a large swan's down tippet which reached to my feet, with my hands in a muff of swan's down big enough for a harlequin to jump through, as was the fashion of the time'. (*Mistress of Charlecote – the Memoirs of Mary Elizabeth Lucy*. Published by Victor Gollancz)

the three points that create a recognizable silhouette of the time for the audience. The feeling of the dresses is light, and the observer is not conscious of a corseted body underneath the cotton petticoat. Contemporary illustrations of these early nineteenth-century women will show a characteristic posture of shoulders and neck promoted by the narrow cut of the dresses across the back of the shoulders, and the flat-heeled slippers.

The basic shape of these high-waisted dresses can be suggested by adjusting a modern pattern for an empire style (high-under-bust-waisted) dress, and taking care to fit the shape of the bodice more closely to the figure, and more narrowly at the back than would be usual in a modern dress. Tricky bodice cutting can be avoided by draping evening dresses over the base of a low-cut bra with skirt attached. It is a mistake to economize by doing without a petticoat, because the lightness of these dresses encourages the inexperienced actress to move with a modern freedom, and even cross her legs beneath the skirt. A cotton petticoat or lining will encourage an appropriate and modest deportment in the wearer, as well as making the dress, however simple, look as if it comes from the past.

The waist dropped gradually throughout the 1830s until it reached a natural position. Bodices were darted in to a slim, but not over-corseted waist, and sleeves and bonnets had grown both in size and decoration to balance the increased size of the skirt. Decoration and ruffles round the bottom of the ankle-length skirts helped them to stand out without the wired or boned underskirts of the following century.

Jackets and Spencers: These short little close-fitting jackets can be made from modern jackets cut short and darted in under the bust. Discard, re-cut or replace the collar, and unpick and refit the centre back seam. Get rid of any shoulder padding, and if necessary, re-cut the armholes or add a wide collar, which will draw attention away from modern seam positions. A generous bonnet bow using wide ribbons can divert attention from a simple neckline. These jackets can create a convincing line over an under-dress that is little more than a long vest shape over a petticoat, and can be quite lightweight.

Overtunics: An overtunic, cut like a full-length tabard and gathered under the bust by a belt or sash, can, with appropriate accessories, be worn over a modern, close-fitting top or body and a full-length skirt, and adequately suggest, with the right accessories, a full period costume. An even simpler option is to use a silk scarf about 3m (10ft) long and ½m (2ft) wide draped round the neck and hanging down to the floor in front. This, with a belt or sash at the correct position, is, of course, historically incorrect, but will nonetheless give the impression of the time to the audience.

Cloaks: Worn as an overcoat, the cloak, with slits for the arms to come through and often with a half-length cape, can be made from two half- or three-quarter-circle cloaks. A miniature cloak, little more than a cape covering the shoulders and with long scarf-like ties reaching to the mid-thighs in front, is a simple-to-make alternative to the Spencer or short jacket mentioned above.

Shawls and scarves: This was a length of cloth 2 or 3m (7 or 10ft) long to cover the shoulders or cross the back and drape loosely and elegantly over the arms. The fashionable young lady studied the elegant wearing of a shawl with deep concern.

Work Clothes
Younger women might reflect the altered waistline in the tying of apron strings, and the

bonnet might replace the cap for high days and holidays, but many older women would have worn clothes cut much like those of their grandmothers. Shawls and cloaks were worn for warmth and can vary from the sack over the shoulders to keep off the rain, through a plaid or woollen blanket-type cloth, to a proper cloth cloak. There are many references in literature to older village women in red wool cloaks. Shoes and boots would have been rougher and clumpier; stockings, when they were worn, thick and hand-knitted. The poorest of all walked barefoot or resorted to clumsy clogs. As always, the way to create a convincing costume for a very poor person is to imagine what you would invent with their resources and in their circumstances. Adults and most children, however poor, wore some sort of head covering when out of doors.

Accessories
Hats, caps, decorative muslin aprons, parasols, fans, muffs, little bags or reticules, gloves and mittens. Jewellery: earrings, lockets, crosses, necklaces, bracelets and brooches were all worn.

Clothes for Men
Heads and Headgear
Hair. Hair was medium length, often curled, sometimes oiled. Most men were clean-shaven but a few wore modest moustaches and sideburns. The grandfather might still cling to the same long powdered hair he had worn in his youth, while his dashing grandson might have the short curly crop reminiscent of a Greek statue.

Top hats: Black, brown, grey or beige, top hats progressed in shape from the wide-brimmed, slightly tapered version in fashion at the end of the eighteenth century to the straight-sided, small-brimmed one of the early and mid-nineteenth century. They were worn by most

of the upper and middle classes. Realistic ones are expensive to buy or hire. They are difficult to make, but cheap versions in several different styles can be bought at fancy dress and party shops, and can be covered in felt to give them more substance.

Round hats: Workers and the lower classes would have worn felt or straw round hats, and these can be recreated from modern hats. A too-crisp silhouette can be softened by holding them over a steaming kettle. Hats of the working classes can be painted or dyed to show marks of wear and weather where appropriate.

Legs and Feet
Shoes, as always, present a major problem, because very little of today's men's footwear resembles that of the past. The quality of his boot leather was a sign of the wealth of the gentleman. The boots so often worn at the time can only be bought from specialist theatrical suppliers, and one of the strongest arguments (when money is in short supply) for dressing actors in long trousers rather than the shorter pantaloons or breeches is that their footwear is largely hidden. A plain elastic-sided or zipped short boot with a lightweight sole is the nearest thing you'll find on the high street. Dancewear shops have more appropriate styles, if you can afford them.

An unfortunate appearance in the drawing room: 'His hair was uncombed; he was in boots, which were covered with mud; his coat seemed to have been designedly immersed in powder, and his universal negligence was not only shabby but uncleanly'. (*Camilla* by Frances Burney, published by The Oxford University Press)

Men of the early nineteenth century.

Clothing the Body

Coats and jackets: The keynote of the gentleman of the time was simple elegance both in cut and colour, though racy young gentlemen might have worn exciting waistcoats or flamboyant colours. The neat-fitting coat worn by all but the very old-fashioned was rather spare in outline: it was cut straight across the front at waist level, and had tails behind which hung down to the knees.

To make these coats by adjusting a modern formal jacket pattern, choose the one with the most vertical seams, and alter them according to your research. Small details will help you create a believable silhouette for the audience: widening the cuffs very slightly into a trumpet shape, cutting the head of the sleeve a few centimetres too big so that you have to gather the top to fit into the armhole, narrowing the shoulders, and cutting the collar more generously. A modern suit jacket can be cut short and fitted close to the waist, and tails cut out of the cloth in the suit trousers. A tailcoat or morning coat can be given a different collar, new buttons or re-cut tails. You may prefer the solution of suggesting the full costume with trousers, shirt, stock and waistcoat and simplifying the women's costume to accord with the less realistic style.

Waistcoats: These were usually of different colour and fabric to the coats, and because of this, they are a valuable resource for the designer and less experienced maker. There were endless variations in cut, but the straight front is the most obvious difference from our waistcoats today. A modern waistcoat front can be re-cut, but it is essential to make sure the trousers are long from crotch to waist so that no puffs of shirt appear between waistcoat bottom and trouser waistband.

Trousers: The most useful shape is fairly close-fitting, very plain and long with a strap under the boot or shoe, though numerous variations appear in fashion illustrations and portraits of the time. It is most important that they are cut higher than modern trousers and are supported by braces rather than a waistband.

Shirts, collars, ties and cravats: The collar was worn high with a cravat, and the gentleman's valet of the time knew the art of tying the perfect cravat. Subtle touches of white, crisp and beautifully laundered linen showed at neck and cuff.

Shirts were white, sometimes with pleated or tucked fronts, though a pale cream or ivory colour gives a better feeling on stage than the aggressive bluish-white of modern polyester. The points of the high collar, which can be added to the neck-band of a modern shirt, were supported by the stock or cravat. Those points ended on the cheeks just below the ears, and this rather fat, linen-bound neck with its high collar is a useful indication of the era when a full costume is outside the range of budget and skill. A strip of white cotton 15cm (6in) wide and 2m (7ft) long wound round the neck will create a stock that both supports the high collar and creates the correct silhouette. Start winding with the middle of the strip at the front of the neck, and cross over the ends at the back. Bring the ends back round to the front, and finish with a bow or a pinned arrangement of folds. Repeat the process with a longer strip if you prefer a fuller effect. A narrower, shorter version in a dark colour will create less rigid stiffening. Cuffs ended in a plain band or a modest frill.

Cloaks: Though both fitted and loose coats were in use, cloaks are a more practical and easily made option. These were full, long, and often cut with an extra cape or two over the shoulders, as well as a large collar. The fastenings, frogs, tasselled cords, buttons and the lining, which was sometimes of contrasting

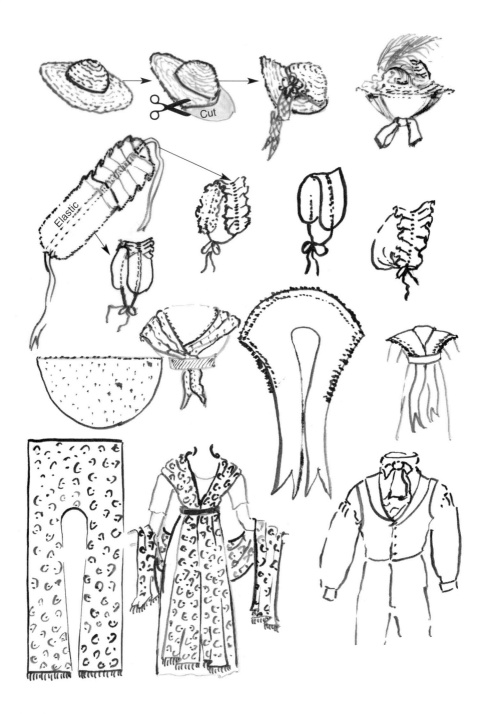

Useful ideas.

coloured silk, created an elaborate effect on what is basically a plain garment.

Work Clothes

Men's trousers became more common than breeches, and coats shorter as the fashion filtered gradually down through the classes. Those engaged in rough work would wear a short coat without tails, and both men and boys working in the country wore smocks with a neckerchief, rather than a cravat. The worker in an office would wear a less elegant version of the more fashionable tailed jacket. Aprons and gaiters were worn according to the needs of the trade. Working men might remove their jackets and work in the waistcoats they wore under them. All men wore hats out of doors, though there are illustrations of men wearing hoods (probably a cut-up sack) as protection from the rain in the fields.

All the signs of young manhood: '… Wellington boots, coat-tail, cravat, down on the upper lip, thoughts of razors, reveries on young ladies, and a new kind of sense of poetry'. (*The Caxtons* by Edward Bulwer Lytton. Published by The Gresham Publishing Company)

Accessories

Hats, walking sticks, gloves, fob watches, shirt studs and perhaps a ring.

Clothes for Children

Children enjoyed a brief respite from the restricting clothes of the previous generation. Girls wore loose cotton and muslin frocks to the ankles, print or plain, with a pinafore for everyday and white with a coloured sash for best. They wore little cotton trousers for warmth and modesty under their ankle length, lightweight skirts. Little boys wore loose-waisted trousers buttoned onto a short jacket, the forerunner of the skeleton suit until, as they approached puberty, they graduated to a tail-less version of their father's clothes. The girls must have been very cold in their light, low-necked dresses, and must have spent much of their playtime bundled up in shawls tied across their chilly little chests. Both boys and girls wore hats, but the hats-out-of-doors rule appears to have been more relaxed at this time. By the time Victoria's rule began, little girls were encased once again in their corsets, petticoats and flounces.

Accessories

Hats, sashes, muffs and shawls for girls; hats, caps and toys for boys.

7 CORSETS, COMMUNICATIONS AND QUEEN VICTORIA 1840–1900

THE LIFE OF THE TIME AND ITS CLOTHES

Queen Victoria's long reign encompasses a period of fashion when clothes reflected, with a seemingly naïve clarity, the ethical and social extremes of the time. The difference between male and female dress became so marked and so tied up (almost literally) with the complex morality of the time that it is difficult not to be both horrified and fascinated by its lack of restraint and subtlety. It is the age of the little woman in her corset and crinoline, weighed down by her petticoats, stepping daintily in the shadow of her strong mate who strode ahead with his sober colours, manly beard and often

nasty habits. Nonetheless, the country and its great empire was ruled by a small, corseted, crinolined and frequently pregnant woman, with a firmness and success belied by her nineteenth-century femininity.

There is much respectability and not a lot of delicacy in the Victorian sense of style. A Victorian lady might appear to float in her flower-like dress of flounces, frills and roses, but under this foaming concoction she would be laced and encased in chemise, knickers, corset, stockings, a crinoline made of horse-hair, linen and many metres of wire, and five or six petticoats. She might be carrying the weight of fifty yards of cloth on her person, not to mention gloves, parasol, fan, shawl and

bonnet; and all this while squeezed so tightly into her corset that she could take only the most shallow of breaths. It is amazing to think that women, in this full rig of the fashionable lady, explored the Amazon, delivered babies and climbed mountains, though unable to mention legs or the lavatory.

The upbringing of the Victorian child was inflexible, and reflected the different attitudes to men and women in its treatment of boys and girls. Of course, the class and financial situation of the child made a difference to its education, and Victorians did not find it inappropriate to sing: 'The rich man in his castle, the poor man at his gate, God made them high and lowly and ordered their estate'. Jesus might have been a carpenter's son from Nazareth, but the Victorian God was white and spoke the Queen's English. Victorians accepted difference in class, and most were untroubled by the notion of social difference and female dependence. God, Queen and Parent as a tripartite example of respectable behaviour, hung heavily over the heads of children of all classes. Heaven and Hell must have seemed under the iron control of all three as, with a board of wood strapped to their back to promote upright carriage, they had their freezing knuckles rapped at piano lessons, or crouched, terrified, in the dark of a coalmine,

Miss Cambell's first party in 1865: 'She was dressed in white muslin with a scarlet sash, and wore a gold chain with a diamond cross at her neck ... and the Duchess in a dress of the richest white silk and fine lace trim'd with bunches of stephanotis and a profusion of diamonds on her head'. (*The Mistress of Charlecote* by Mary Elizabeth Lucy, introduction by Alice Fairfax-Lucy, published by Victor Gollancz)

opening doors for dragon-rattling coaltrucks to earn a penny for their desperate families.

The difference in income and education, and consequently the lifestyle of different classes, was staggering. Upper-class women needed to marry, and the schooling of their early years, and of course their dress, prepared them to attract suitable men and to be un-questioning and moral wives and mothers of the future rulers of the British Empire. The accepted way for a lady to earn money was to marry it. The music-hall song about the bird in a gilded cage, a young lady 'whose beauty was sold for an old man's gold', was sung onstage by a less classy beauty, who probably sold her own beauty for the same old man's gold but without the marriage lines. The poorer women struggled to feed their huge families, and children started work as young as five or six years of age. About half of all children died in their first five years, and many more before they grew up.

When young Victoria came to the throne, the railway was about to effect a dramatic improvement in communications. The industrial revolution brought hungry people from the country to the crowded, foul-smelling towns in search of a better living. Anyone who could afford to do more than scrabble to stay alive aimed for respectability. Artists, writers, social reformers and wonderful inventions and innovations grew sturdily through the weeds to help them achieve this goal. The list is impressive: the postage stamp, the telegraph, the telephone, national and local newspapers, disinfectant, a countrywide police force, the telephone and the motorcar. Education, some-what shakily, became compulsory. Great Britain ruled the waves and the enormous Empire. But the poor were still very poor, and the rich very rich.

The correct and fashionable Victorian lady wasn't supposed to think for herself – and indeed how could she, when she was faint from tight lacing and trained from childhood to be seen and not heard. Her all-powerful husband, so much more comfortable in his shirt, trousers, waistcoat and jacket, had to make all the running. Her duty was to him, and his to his country. To us he might appear bound up in his high collar and cravat, his voluminous shirt-tails wound round his bottom and thighs under his trousers; he might seem burdened with his hat, stick and gloves. But compare his freedom of body with that of his trussed-up wife.

Of course, all this fashionable equipment required money. And servants to brush the mud of the filthy streets off those huge skirts, and refurbish the hats and boots after every shower. The footman or coachman would wear a uniform provided by his employer; the appearance of their servants was an important accessory to the lady and gentleman of the house. The society woman needed the help of a maid to accomplish the lengthy and complicated business of dressing and undressing, and the many daily changes of outfit demanded by the etiquette of the time. Her female servants dressed according to the taste of their mistress, and lengths of cloth or aprons were often given as presents to these women, which must have felt a bit like being given school uniform for a birthday present.

It is important to remember that not everyone would have followed the fashion of the time, though all would have felt its influence. Most women's and children's clothes were made at home by the women who wore them, and this must have resulted in some quite rough and ready cutting, given the complication of cut reflected in the portraits of the time. Clothes were refurbished, altered, and turned (taken apart and re-made inside out) when they faded, and they were often dyed black, to serve as the mourning dress heralded by the death of a relative. Those with less money would either try to copy the costly style of high society, or wear outdated, clumsy, or just convenient and affordable clothes.

Pictures of Victorian costume, and examples in costume collections, show us that clothes hid the natural man and woman. The lady's waist is small; her shoulders slope; her skirt is wide; her legs are invisible, as is the true shape of her restrained body – it would not be easy for her to run or bend. The gentleman is tall, his height often emphasized by a top hat. His silhouette is straight, and without unnatural additions to shoulders; his stiff collar, neatly cut clothes and sober neckwear give an impression of confidence, moral rectitude and authority. The difference between the respectable, if plain clothes of the middle classes, and the desperate poverty of the penniless, was considerable. Towards the end of the century there are signs of woman wanting to emerge from her subservient role: this is evident in the less cumbersome dress, particularly in costume for sporting activity.

The rich – Lord Frederick Verisopht '... exhibited a suit of clothes of the most superlative cut, a pair of whiskers of similar quality, a moustache, a head of hair and a young face'. ... *the solvent* – '... The expected swain arrived with his hair very damp from recent washing; and a clean shirt, whereof the collar might have belonged to some giant ancestor, forming, together with a white waistcoat of similar dimensions, the chief ornament of his person'. ... *and the poor* – 'Although he was eighteen or nineteen years old, he wore a skeleton suit such as is usually put upon very little boys in the arms and legs ... most absurdly short ... round his neck was a tattered child's frill, only half concealed by a coarse man's neckerchief'. (*Nicholas Nickleby* by Charles Dickens, published by Penguin Books)

CREATING THE CLOTHES FOR THE STAGE

Clothes for Women

Heads and Headgear

Hair: The fashionable head was small and neat. Women's hair was not cut, and was worn up when they made the change from schoolgirl to young and marriageable woman. The simple way to achieve this is to part the hair neatly in the centre and put it in a bun at the back. If the hair is short it can be 'glued' into shape with mousse, wax or gel, and a false bun or ringlets attached to the back. If there is no hair to anchor the false bun, the short hair could be disguised with a small cap or snood which looks as if it is full of hair. Any hair hanging down should be curled. False ringlets can be glued onto combs or clips.

Make-up: It was not considered respectable for Victorian woman to wear make-up.

Bonnets: Women of all classes wore hats out of doors, and often indoors when they were outside their own homes, and the bonnet was the most usual daytime hat. Its shape changed throughout the era, but it is a clear way of signalling to the audience that the actors are playing Victorian women. The basic shape of the bonnet can be copied using today's hats: quite a convincing base can be made by trimming the brim off the back of a felt or straw wide-brimmed hat, and shaping the sides by means of ribbons under the chin. However, it can be more convenient to use chin elastic to do the shaping, and disguise it with decorative ribbons. Bonnets were trimmed with ribbons, flowers, feathers and veils, and were sometimes worn over little muslin or silk caps, which showed lace or ruffles nestling under the brim of the bonnet.

Caps: Little white muslin or silk caps, plain or trimmed with lace or ruffles, were worn by all classes of women, though they would be covered by a bonnet out of doors. These caps provide a useful way of dressing the Victorian head onstage, as they can conceal the fact that an actress has short hair and thus save the expense and inconvenience of a wig. The pretty, gauzy ruffles and pastel bows of a young lady, the plain starched cotton of the maid, and the grubby coarse calico mobcap of the slattern, can point up a character with economy and precision. Many variations can be made using the coif or the mobcap as a starting point.

Sun bonnets: A soft cloth bonnet in coloured or print cotton, designed to keep the sun off the back of the neck and to shade the face, was worn by children and working women. These can be pretty or coarse according to the cloth, and do not have the ladylike connotations that a modern audience receives from the sight of an actress in a long skirt and a shaped bonnet.

The boater: Worn straight on the head and not tipped back, the boater was favoured in the latter half of the period by sporting or more emancipated women. It was trimmed with a plain band of ribbon, but not usually with flowers or fanciful decoration.

Decorated combs or hair slides: Small hair-combs or hair slides can be decorated with

A woman's hair was her 'crowning glory': '... a crown of thick plaits behind, and in front the longest, the glossiest curls I ever saw. She was dressed in pure white; an amber-coloured scarf was passed over her shoulder and across her breast, tied at the side, and descending in long, fringed ends below her knee'. (*Jane Eyre* by Charlotte Brontë, published by William Clowes Ltd)

Victorian women.

feathers, flowers or ribbons to adorn the hair for a ball. They can also prove a useful disguise for the additions of false curls and ringlets.

Legs and Feet

White, light-coloured and black stockings were worn, and modern opaque tights can cover most theatrical Victorian legs, as they will scarcely be seen under the long skirts. For rougher or more rural characters, if the stockings show, make them thick ones out of jersey cloth or even the sleeves of knitted sweaters. They need not have feet if the characters are wearing boots – they can be a tube with a loop of elastic under the heel inside the shoe, and kept up with a garter above the knee.

Lightweight black boots for day wear, or court shoes in pastel colours to go with evening dress, will give the impression of the correct shoe. Try to give the classier characters a slight heel, as it will help actors to achieve a more convincing walk, particularly if they are used to wearing trainers. Small feet and delicacy were fashionable – clumping boots and thick shoes belong to poorer or very rural characters. Bare feet meant abject poverty, and ill-fitting boots and bare legs also give out a strong message.

Clothing the Body

Dresses: Throughout the Victorian era the emphasis was on unnaturally small waists. Sleeves varied in size, from the very slim and neat, to huge puffs. The violent alterations of the skirt width that occurred throughout this period might seem to be a forerunner of the violent alterations in length that occurred in the following century. Young Queen Victoria ascended the throne in a wide skirt, and throughout her long reign the fashionable woman widened it, widened it still further, drew the fullness to the back, narrowed it to a slim hourglass and sent it out into a bell shape

again. But the slim waist in its natural position remained fashionable throughout all the billowings and shrinkings of the skirt it supported. Generally the neck was high in the day, and low in the evening. Victorian women wore corsets, so the basic costume must somehow suggest a corseted shape, even if skill and budget are insufficient to provide one.

Ladies' dresses, with their carefully fitted bodices, elaborate sleeves and voluminous skirts, together with the undergarments to support them, clearly require a great deal of cloth and skilful fitting. A modern dress, made for a bride or a ball, will not give the same impression, particularly if several characters are to be dressed and a hotchpotch of styles results. It is better to find another way, perhaps using a basic costume with accessories, to suggest the time. The stretchy, close-fitting tops, bodices and leotards available today are a possible way to suggest this shape without complicated cutting. For upper-class women, use long-sleeved tops for day, and short-sleeved or sleeveless for evening. Try to keep the shape close to the Victorian silhouette, and keep it simple so that any embellishments or accessories you add give a clear message. As the characters descend the social scale, a smooth fit becomes less important and bulgy, ill-fitting, makeshift clothes will give a good indication of the meagre budget of the wearer. Shawls are useful, and a simple triangle of either ragged or opulent cloth over a long skirt will say a lot with great simplicity.

'Farmers and farmers' wives in their Sunday suits and bonnets and shawls; old dames in red cloaks gossiping together; and then beautiful Miss Vivian Herbert, with the loveliest white gown and lace parasol. ...' (From *Little Lord Fauntleroy* by Francis Hodgson Burnett, published by Penguin Books)

It is next to impossible to suggest this time in a short skirt or trousers, so the horrible and expensive truth is, you have to find some way of getting long skirts for the women in your company. The Victorian skirt varied from vast quantities of cloth gathered onto the tiny waistband and draped over crinoline and petticoats, to a slimmer, flatter-fronted tulip shape at the end of the century. If you do have to resort to the desperate measure of using modern long skirts, it is better to keep it as the simple statement of a long skirt, and not try to dress it up with frills and braid. A full-length gathered or circular skirt will prove its worth over and over again in many different eras.

Shawls and cloaks: Coats and jackets were worn, but so were shawls and cloaks, and these are a much easier and more adaptable costume option. A simple triangle 1.5m (5ft) square is a marvellous empty canvas for the costumier to paint the character of its wearer. Cream- or pastel-fringed silk or a light paisley wool for a young lady, black crepe bordered with black sateen for a sad widow, moth-eaten brown or grey jersey for the hungry pauper, red satin folded to reveal the breasts for the harlot, and coloured wool folded warmly across the chest for the dear old lady, are all obvious examples. The circular cloak can be adapted or decorated to create outer garments that echo the many different styles invented by the ingenious Victorian dressmaker.

The corset: Corset-making is a tricky business. A simplified basic corset pattern has been included in Chapter 10 for those who are eager to try, and more information can be found in the books recommended in the bibliography.

Work Clothes
The Victorian clung to an appearance of respectability as long as possible, but as always when poverty gets a hold, the most pressing need is for food and warmth. The long skirt, however threadbare and dirty, and the bonnet, however rudimentary, were fundamental to a Victorian woman's self respect. Clothes of the poor have less sense of shape, style and smoothness, and become mere coverings for the body. There are many illustrations and cartoons of women wearing lumpy crinolines for most inappropriate work. Workers in refined employment – such as governesses, teachers and shop workers – wore a modest, quiet-coloured and undecorated version of the fashionable dress of the time.

Accessories
Hats, gloves, shawls, fichus, sashes, jewellery, fans, veils, parasols.

Clothes for Men
Heads and Headgear
Hair: Men wore moustaches and side-whiskers, and if you can contact your cast early enough, ask them not to have haircuts, and to grow facial hair; provide them with pictures of suitable styles so that they know what to aim for. Hair can be parted at the side or in the middle, and kept that way with lacquer or gel. Avoid fringes and hair flopping over the forehead for any character with aspirations to urbanity.

Hats: The hat is such an important part of Victorian costume that it is worth taking a great deal of trouble to provide one. No man, whatever his age or class, went out without a hat, and men took off their hats indoors.

The top hat: Cheap versions of top hats and bowler hats, which suggest the Victorian ones, are sold in novelty and party shops for dressing up. They are often brightly coloured or silver, but it is possible to use them as a base and to cover them with felt or papier mâché and paint. Modern top hats are too low to be

Victorian men.

accurate for the time, but create an excellent impression if you can get hold of them; few audience members will distinguish between different shapes of top hat.

The bowler: Bowlers can be found from the same sources as top hats, and can be painted to imitate the beige and brown bowlers that could be worn in the country. Black ones were worn with more formal dress.

The boater: This was worn for informal summer and sporting occasions.

The round hat: A round felt or straw hat was worn by rural country folk, and these can be adapted from modern hats. They protected the face from sun or bad weather in the fields, and less battered versions were sometimes worn by more affluent men on extremely informal occasions.

The cap: A peaked cloth cap was worn mostly by working men and boys.

Legs and Feet
Socks were inconspicuous, though a fashionable young man might wear brightly coloured ones. Make sure that bare leg does not show over the top of a too-short sock when the actor

---

Alice Liddell recollects her 1860s' childhood: 'Mr Dodgson [Lewis Carroll] always wore black clergyman's clothes in Oxford, but when he took us out on the river, he used to wear white flannel trousers. He also replaced his black top hat by a hard, white straw hat on these occasions, but of course retained his black boots because in those days white tennis shoes had never been heard of'. (*The Cornhill Magazine*, July 1932)

---

sits down onstage, unless you particularly want the audience to notice the sock.

The most useful modern shoe for this time is the Chelsea boot (a short ankle boot with elastic or zip at the side). It is sometimes possible to find skating boots and unscrew the skates: you will be left with a narrow, low-heeled, lace-up boot that you can dye or paint if necessary. Streets were filthy and full of horse dung, and country lanes were muddy or dusty, and it took a great deal of care to show a clean pair of boots to the world if you had no servants to clean them for you.

Clothing the Body
The frock coat: This was a square-fronted jacket, not an overcoat, which finished around or just above the knee; it was seen on all classes of men in its various states of smartness or decrepitude. It presents a problem to the in-experienced costume tailor because there is no modern equivalent except the rather thin and unconvincing versions made sometimes for today's weddings, or the uniform coats of doormen at some smart hotels. Nevertheless, a modern, well-fitted jacket pattern can be adapted in collar and length to make a convincing reproduction, particularly to represent the rougher, thicker versions for country workers.

The morning coat: This is the shape worn at formal weddings today, though the Victorian version was more shaped to the figure. A modern frock coat will look more convincing if braided in a matching colour (usually black or grey) round the edges and round the collar to give it extra weight.

The short jacket: This was a mid-thigh-length, less formal jacket, often with a rounded front. If you use a modern coat or jacket, you may want to add an extra button and buttonhole at the top to make a four-buttoned, higher-collared line, and re-cut the bottom of the front of the jacket to a different shape. Some of these jackets were braided round the edge. Other modern jackets and short coats of an unusual or unfamiliar shape can look to the audience as if they come from an earlier period when combined with Victorian rather than modern accessories. A shorter, hip- or waist-length, loose-fitting jacket was sometimes worn by working men and boys.

Evening tails: Evening tails – the high-fronted, back-tailed black 'penguin' suit that is still worn with a white tie and waistcoat on very formal occasions today – has changed very little since the mid-nineteenth century. Consequently tails are worth searching for and hoarding against a future ball scene. Evening tails or morning coats, if you can get hold of them, may not be historically accurate, but will give an impression of careful formality belonging to a past age.

Waistcoats: Men and boys wore waistcoats under their jackets, and these went through many minor transformations while remaining a short, sleeveless jacket with pockets. Modern waistcoats can have the points at the front turned in and stitched to make a straight-fronted one, and the buttons altered. Collars can be added. It is easy to alter a waistcoat down the back seam, and a well fitting waistcoat will help the actor and the audience to get a feeling of the past. When a waistcoat is too long for the actor, it is sometimes possible to shorten it at the shoulders, thus creating a high-buttoned, short-waisted effect.

Trousers: Trousers should be fairly close fitting, they should cover the top of the shoes, and should narrow towards the bottom, or at least not flap wildly; they should not have stitched seams like jeans. It often works to have trousers that are a bit too big, and suspend them on braces. Rough or country characters can tuck the bottom of their baggier trousers into boots and wear belt and braces. It is essential, if the character is supposed to look well dressed, that trousers are cut high enough at the waist for the waistband to be hidden under the waistcoat; a gap that reveals the shirt between trouser and waistcoat indicates a man either too busy or too poor to care about his personal appearance.

Shirts, collars and ties: The shirt, collar and tie will help to make the picture convincing. Shirt collars should fit closely and may be turned up and re-cut to a high straight shape, or to a short pointed turnover, or the points turned down to make a wing collar. The cravats and bows of the early years of the time were varied by the knotted tie, more like those of today, in the later years of the century. The shirts of the gentry were usually white, and crisp collars and cuffs were the mark of a gentleman, or at least of a man who worked in a clean, and therefore more gentrified, job. Working men could wear striped or coloured shirts, often with the detachable collar removed, the neck open, and a neckerchief knotted round the neck rather than a tie.

Work Clothes
The rough dress of the agricultural worker and the very poor remained largely unchanged. The aprons, gaiters and other accessories that protected clothes and bodies from wear can be imagined from an understanding of the tasks performed by the men. Rural workers wore smock-frocks made of unbleached linen, with the fullness controlled by smocking. Men in clerical or office jobs wore cheaper versions of the stiff collar, suits and hats of the gentry. The distinction in cut and fit must be quite clearly marked so that the audience registers the difference in the characters' financial situation. Trouser and

Useful ideas.

cuff length, shoes and boots, crispness of linen, colour and texture, all point up this difference; but the most distinguishing feature of the costume will be the way the actor wears it. Men in service in the big country houses wore livery and uniforms that reflected the status of their masters.

Accessories
Hats, walking sticks, gloves, watch chains and discrete jewellery.

Clothes for Children

Victorian children were encased in layers of heavy clothes; even babies were covered in heavy, sticky, starched frills. Girls, laced into corsets to promote a small waist in later life, froze bare-necked in winter, and boiled in their layers of petticoats in summer. Very young boys were dressed in skirts, but this tends to confuse a modern audience. Little boys wore knickerbockers or breeches below the knee. The Eton suit, with its short dark jacket and long trousers, grew out of the skeleton suit and remained formal boys' wear for years. Boys were decked up in mock uniforms or heavy serge suits until the relative freedom of the sailor suit became fashionable.

Little girls wore their hair down, and put on hats or bonnets out of doors. Girls were allowed to show their ankles until they put up their hair. Use a calf-length full skirt with a close-fitting, round-necked top and perhaps a frilly white collar and hair-ribbon bow. Pina-fores protected the dress for school or play. Bonnets can be made by re-cutting the brims of modern straw or felt hats, and adding ribbons. A school blazer, its pocket and badge removed,

or a small woman's jacket, can be re-cut at the hem and taken in at the sides to make a version of the short jacket. It will suggest the period if you use a close-fitting, high-necked jersey and leggings, or close-fitting trousers cut off below the knee. The addition of a white collar, frilled or plain, and a neckbow and hat, will underline your message. The sailor suit, popular for both boys with trousers or knickerbockers and for girls with skirts, can be suggested by a sailor collar and round straw hat. Both boys and girls can wear opaque black tights onstage, though coloured and striped stockings were worn as well; they would have lightweight shoes or short lace-up boots.

Children whose parents could afford it wore clothes made especially for them. The poorer children wore cut-down adult clothes, bare legs, and ill-fitting shoes or bare feet. This look can be achieved by rough-cutting modern clothes to the right size. Again the use of hats or caps shows the time.

Accessories
Hats, gloves, sashes and muffs for girls, hat and gloves for boys and toys of the time for both.

Little girls at a harsh school uniformly dressed: '... in brown dresses, made high, and surrounded by a narrow tucker about the throat, with little pockets of holland (shaped something like a highlander's purse) tied in front of their frocks, and designed to serve the purpose of a workbag'. (*Jane Eyre* by Charlotte Brontë, published by William Clowes Ltd)

8 FROM DRAWING ROOM TO BATTLEFIELD 1900–1945

THE LIFE OF THE TIME AND ITS CLOTHES

The rich were still very rich and the poor very poor, but change was in the air. During the next fifty years the grip of the aristocracy as leaders of fashion began to loosen its hold on clothes, as well as on the country. Women were at last able to retain the property and wealth they brought to a marriage, and were discovering a public voice of their own. The shock of two world wars, which presented women with the necessity of doing what had been men's work, and the connections, welcome or unwelcome, it gave Britain with Europe and North America, opened the door. The female silhouette reflected this change.

Fashionable women began the century corseted from bust to thigh. An opulent bust, often padded under the arms and enhanced by 'bust improvers', was laced into a tiny waist, which in turn swelled into a curved and luscious (and also 'improved') bottom. The dress exaggerated the outline, with elaborate bodice fronts and flat-fronted, back-pleated skirts. The silhouette was blatantly provocative but apparently respectable, like the morals of the upper classes led by Victoria's son, the naughty, party-loving Edward VII.

Men's clothes relaxed a little – shoulders were less tight, and the dinner jacket replaced the tailcoat for less formal evening occasions. But no man went out without a hat, and few gentlemen without gloves and a walking cane. And to be incorrectly dressed was unthinkable – twirl your moustache as you may, if you didn't know the rules, you weren't fit for the best society! The rules for the correct dress for a

sporting country-house party were every bit as strict as those for a box at the opera.

Upper-class children were tucked away up in their nurseries with Nanny unless called for by their parents, the girls being educated to be suitably married and the boys to rule the empire. Their dress still echoed that of the adults, though the sailor suit gave them more freedom of movement. Girls' skirts were calf-length until they left the schoolroom for the ballroom, and little boys progressed from baby skirts to short trousers to knickerbockers or breeches, and thence to long trousers.

Life was changing for the working classes and for women; slowly, but they were changing. Slums were being improved, and many children who would have been completely uneducated in the previous century could go to the free schools. It began to be accepted in a wider section of society that women had minds of their own and could coexist with men

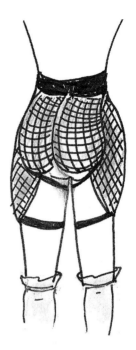

Added enhancement for the more opulent hips required by the Edwardian lady of fashion.

in education at work as well as at home. The 'angel in the house' was rattling her corset bones and loosening her stays.

Little boys in slums still played bare-footed and even bare-bottomed in open sewers, and closely chaperoned young ladies in drawing rooms prayed desperately for husbands as their only escape from hopeless spinsterhood and Mama. But the middle classes forged ahead. By 1900 the House of Commons had overtaken the House of Lords as the dominant chamber in Parliament, and quite respectable girls went out to quite respectable jobs echoing male fashion in their tailor-made tweeds that differed only in quality and cut from those of their aristocratic counterparts.

Corsets softened, waists and hemlines rose, women's necks were freed from those high stiff collars; ankles peeped out, and then came

The rich: ... An Edwardian boy of seven or eight off to boarding school: 'Until today Hugh had worn the clothes of a little boy: jerseys with kilt or shorts, and sailor suits for special occasions. Now he was dressed as a schoolboy in a Knickerbocker suit with Eton collar and tie. Above him on the rack lay his overcoat and bowler hat'. (*The Children of the House* by Brian Fairfax-Lucy and Philippa Pearce; published by Longmans Young Books, 1968)

And the poor: ...'The shirt I wear to bed is the shirt I wear to school. I wear it day in, day out. It's the shirt for football, for climbing walls, for robbing orchards ... I go to mass in that shirt, and people sniff the air and move away. The respectable boys ... wear tweed jackets, warm woollen sweaters, shirts, ties and shiny new boots'. (*Angela's Ashes* by Frank McCourt, published by Harper Collins)

boldly into the open as women fought for their right to vote. The men left home for the terrible slaughter of World War I, and the women, often with a sense of liberation, perforce took over many of their roles. Those men that returned found a new, boyish woman, corsetless, short-haired, short-skirted and voting. In the years of peace that followed, skirts rose to the knee and both men's and women's dress became less restricting. Men's costume, always slower to change than women's, echoed this new ease with softer hats and less structured suits. The sporting outfits invented for the pastimes of the idle rich influenced a new freedom in the everyday clothes of the less wealthy.

Classes may have joined together to win the war, but the post-war years brought back intense social divisions. The rich – beaded and angular-bodied – flashed their knees dancing the exuberant Charleston, and the desperate miners went on strike to buy food for their starving, threadbare children. An explosion of new delights hit London, burying for many the financial problems of the 1930s, and radiated throughout the country. It was a time of intense artistic creativity. The modernist culture, with its worrying cubists, its exotic ballets, its complex poets and un-frilly architecture may have been resisted by society, which hankered for a past it knew and understood, but fashion soaked it up, as it always has done and will do, with blithe and brave unconcern. Waists were 'in', and bias-cut glamour skimmed slim hips: furs in winter and suntans in summer: and cinemas and magazines spread the latest fashion news to all.

And then, in 1939, another war. Cloth became more difficult to buy, and women's work called for convenience and authority. Waste and luxury were unpatriotic, and the square-shouldered jacket and just-below-knee-length skirt gave crisp lines to the female body whether in or out of the uniforms of national service. Summer dresses created the same neat, businesslike shape. Trousers were worn by women in all walks of life, and lost the risqué image of the previous decade. Rationing meant altering, adapting and re-cutting old clothes to make new, and many a wedding dress was made out of the lace curtains. Hats became small and neat to complement the new silhouette. The fashionable man was the man in uniform – and for many working men, their uniforms were better than the best Sunday best suits they had ever had.

The clothes, and most particularly the female clothes, of the first half of the twentieth century provide us with a precise record of the huge social changes occurring in the lifestyle. How could a woman in her early twenties in 1900, who revealed her ankles only in the privacy of her bedroom or the glimpsing twirl of a waltz, have imagined her daughter going to a 1920s ball in a chemise that showed her knees, and her granddaughter wearing trousers and working side by side with men?

The exaggerated curves of the women at the beginning of the period were achieved by strongly boned corsets that prevented a natural movement of the body. The high collars were also boned, and hats wide and heavy. It required considerable practice to sustain the arched back and high chin, control a train, balance the hat and manage the petticoats, and a girl's body had to be trained to move gracefully within such restrictions before taking her place in the ballroom. Consequently elegant deportment was a badge of gentility, as none but the rich had the time or money to teach their children these unnatural movements. Educating the female mind took second place in most schoolrooms.

Women began to move towards a life where marriage was not the only possible career, and their clothes became less restrictive. Skirts revealed first the ankle, then the calf. The corseted waist, which had tyrannized women for the preceding hundred years, was vanquished, or at least disempowered for a time; the shapeless dresses of the 1920s concealed women's figures as they marched or danced towards enfranchisement. The right to vote achieved, fashion showed off a new, confident woman with flair and daring. The sexy elegance of the 1930s was replaced by shoulders squared with padding, and women took their place beside men in World War II.

Men's clothes changed less dramatically, but the rigid lines that went with the empire-building and family-controlling attitude gradually relaxed. Suits changed in detail, rather than in essence, and the unstarched collar was as much a revolution in its discrete way as the uncorseted waist. The sports jacket worn with trousers and waistcoat of a different cloth was a relaxation of formality that heralded a new ease in the strict etiquette so fundamental to Edwardian life. To look at a photograph of a couple in 1900, so bound in their clothes, and a couple only half a century later, both perhaps wearing trousers and jerseys, is to understand the phenomenal change in attitude and clothes of this extraordinary era.

The importance of feeling you look right for an occasion was the same then as now: '... Lady B. ... has on an admirable black two-piece garment, huge mink collar, perfectly brand new pair of white gloves, exquisite shoes and stockings, and tiny little black-white-red-blue-orange hat, intrinsically hideous but producing the effect of extreme smartness and elegance.

Am instantly aware that my hair is out of curl, that I have not powdered my nose for hours, that my shoes – blue suede – bear no relation whatever to my dress – grey tweed – and that Aunt Blanche ... is in her old mauve cardigan'. (*The Provincial Lady in Wartime* E. M. Delafield, published by Virago)

In fifty years, Britain and the clothes of its people, particularly its women, had changed with unprecedented speed. The constricted lady, swathed from throat to ankle in rustling silk and frilled petticoats, freed her swaying, S-shaped body and emerged, only a few steps behind her man, changed and crystallized into the neat-outlined, quick-stepping, post-war woman ready for the second Elizabethan age.

CREATING THE CLOTHES FOR THE STAGE

Clothes for Women

Heads and Headgear

Hair: For the first ten years of the century women wore their hair long and swept up into wide and elaborate styles shaped rather like an onion. No woman with any self-respect (those with bohemian tendencies excepted!) wore her hair down after she had outgrown the schoolroom. The easiest way to achieve an acceptable shape is to ask the actress to wind her hair into a loose bun on the top of her head and then to bend over so that her head is almost upside-down; when she is upright again it will fall into the right meringue-like shape. In time the shape became less full, and by 1920 many fashionable women cut their hair, an action that had been unthinkable to many for over a hundred years, and wore it with a parting, or curled. To many women though, particularly in less fashionable or emancipated circles, a girl's hair remained her crowning glory, though it was invariably worn up if longer than shoulder length. One of the hallmarks of the 1930s is the small, neat head perched on a long neck, and an effort should be made to create this with careful hairdressing and a line that shows the neck to its best advantage. In the stringent war years of the 1940s, hair, at least, was unrationed and women enjoyed it. It was drawn up at the sides with combs or grips, rolled back from the

Women in the first half of the twentieth century.

forehead and curled above the collar – you might not be able to have a new dress, but you could have an elaborate hairstyle, and women did.

The working classes followed the fashions set by those with more leisure, but it should be remembered that it is always young people who pursue fashion most avidly, and many older women would have retained the long hair and bun of the preceding century.

Make-up: The damning Edwardian phrase 'They say she paints!' referred not to the subject's artistic work, but to the use of powder and rouge. To the post-Edwardian, make-up was no longer a proclamation of loose morals or secret desperation and it was worn with open relish, though initially it shocked the older generation. By 1940 most young women wore make-up. The familiarity of today's theatre audience with films of the twentieth century makes it easy to recognize the make-up of the women, and it is a useful and relatively cheap aid to setting a period onstage.

Edwardian hats: These were elaborate, high at first and wide later, and always much decorated with feathers, quills, bows, flowers and sometimes even stuffed birds or butterflies. They can be created from the wider straw and felt hats of today. A 5cm (2in) border or frill round the brim will create a surprising difference to the impression of width, as will added decoration to the crown to the height.

Felt hats: The many and rapidly changing shapes of felt hats can be recreated by remodelling today's felt hats. The close-fitting little hats of the 1920s worn low on the forehead, the small angled hats of the 1930s, and the forward tilted and often military styles of the 1940s, owe much of their period look to the way they are worn. Even the genuine article will look wrong if the hat is worn at the wrong angle.

Straw hats: Straw summer hats were worn all through the period, and followed the shape and angle of wear of other hats of the time, though they tended to have wider brims.

The turban hat: Turban hats can be created in 1920s style, with a small, straight scarf tied round the head as a bandeau; in 1930s style, from a long, narrow, bias-cut scarf wound closely round the head with the end tucked in neatly; or in 1940s style, by folding a square headscarf into a triangle, wrapping it round the head, tying the two ends in front, and tucking the third corner in the knot. In all three cases the colour pattern and texture of the cloth, and the elegance or clumsiness of its tying, will give clues to the audience about the character in a simple and economical form.

The beret: The shape of the beret has remained unchanged – the angle it is worn at, and the hairstyle beneath it, can put it in the past.

Legs and Feet
Stockings: Women's skirts during this period shortened to show their legs, and so stockings, now they were on view, gained a new importance. Black, white or pastel-coloured while

Two girls address the problem of getting ready for a clandestine assignation: 'We must get hold of some powder and rouge'. These commodities were utterly forbidden by Uncle Matthew, who liked to see female complexions in a state of nature, and often pronounced that paint was for whores and not for his daughters. 'We can blue our eyelids out of Jassy's paintbox'. (From *The Pursuit of Love*, Nancy Mitford, published by Penguin Books)

Stockings: '... they laid in Sido's hands, two silk stockings as heavy and cold as a pair of little snakes'. *Stockings from around 1900*: 'The silk stockings and the slim-toed shoes betray women's stubborn determination not to abandon their costly, unreasonable, un-seasonable fashions'. *Stockings in the winter of 1941*: '... whether natural silk or not, a pair of stockings today is composed of no more than eight to ten grams of thread. A frail protection against rain and tempest ...'. *Stockings from around 1945*: Colette, *Paris de ma Fenêtre*, published by Martin Secker and Warburg Ltd

skirts were long, and then in pale or flesh tones, they had a seam at the back and were more or less opaque until the thinner silk and artificial silk ones of the thirties and forties arrived in Britain.

Shoes: The fashionable foot for the whole of this period was small and narrow. The shape of the female foot was usually emphasized by a built-up heel, and it is essential to use lightweight, neatly structured and well-fitting shoes or boots if you hope to give an impression of elegance to women of the first half of this century. A clumpy rubber sole will force the actor to walk in a way that will destroy any impression of period, and footwear that feels and looks suitably 'in period' will help any performance. Working boots and shoes were strong and waterproof, with heavy soles. Sturdy design and effective mending would have been more important than good fitting. Re-create in the stage shoe or boot the heavy, rugged and often battered appearance of working boots and shoes if the character of the role demands it.

Clothes for the Body
Until around 1915, corsets still shaped the figure, and any costume suggesting this time must pay tribute to the restricting nature of its fashion. Corsets were softer and waists higher after 1910, but the shape was still unnatural. Corsets or boned under-bodices of various types are still made today for the fashion industry, but they will not create the currently unfashionable curves of the Edwardian beauty. If the making of a corset is outside your skill, it may be possible to add boning to an existing garment of the right shape. Another and more successful alternative is to make a shaped, boned waistband to be worn over a blouse or close-fitting top. These waist-bands, which should fit closely to the curves of the body and can be quite wide, will give an impression of richness and formality. They will be most effective when used on a simplified version of period costume, and the message stands out clearly. A ribbon choker round the neck will convey the feeling of those high Edwardian collars.

That tiny waist, which had tormented women's bodies, obsessed every fashionable mind, and governed fashion for the preceding hundred years, rose briefly and then dropped to the hips. By the early 1920s the ideal body was flat-busted and slim-hipped, and the uncurved line between the two hid the waist entirely. The simple lines of this time make it relatively easy to suggest with adaptations of modern clothes or a simple tunic shape. This

Putting on the corset: '... then the lacing would follow, beginning at the waist and travelling gradually up and down, until the necessary proportions had been achieved. The silk laces and their tags would fly out under the maid's deft fingers, with the flick of a skilled worker mending a net'. (From *The Edwardians* by Vita Sackville West, published by The Hogarth Press)

Women in the first half of the twentieth century.

can be dressed with the many accessories of the time: beads, brooches and bags, furs and belts, sashes at hip level, gloves and hats – all these help to create a picture. It is important to remember that poorer communities and those further from urban centres would still wear the fashions of the past, and that older people adopt new fashions less readily than the young ones. At a party in 1926 a girl might show her knees in a little beaded dress smaller than a middle-aged countrywoman's vest.

The exuberance and childlike freedom of the 1920s vanished when the waist returned in the 1930s. The fashionable shape was long, lean and rather square-shouldered. The rather mannish tailored suits reaching to mid-calf in winter tweeds, and the summer dresses and separates, can be recreated from modern clothes provided the skirts are long enough. The hats, gloves, bags and shoes, and particularly furs, will give the audience a strong message.

Much can be done with blouses. Try to find a shape with shoulders that look right, and alter the cuffs and neck to give an impression of the time. Evening dresses were sophisticated and openly sexy. They clung to the body, bared the back and twitched into flowing fishtails or ruffles at the hem. The urbane party-goer wreathed in cigarette smoke and trailing furs and glamour strolled through the nightclubs with an open confidence in her sexuality that had hitherto belonged to the courtesan. The

artistically inclined discussed life in clothes influenced by the East or the vibrant colours of the Russian ballet, and country cousins tried their best to keep up with the changing fashions of this exciting era.

The variety of style in the 1930s makes it possible to imitate the fashions with modern clothes, though it requires great attention to skirt length and detail of accessories, hair and make-up if the picture is to convince.

The same is true of the clothes of the 1940s, particularly as skirts were shorter as rationing limited the amount of cloth available. The ingenuity of women in remodelling and adding collars, cuffs and so on to old clothes can be echoed by the costume designer. Again the make-up, hair, stockings and shoes will give the picture, and although the suit or dress may not be accurate in cut, the correct length and waistline, a suitable cloth and the right accessories, hairstyle and make-up will give the audience a picture they recognize.

Work Clothes
Young and fashion-conscious working women followed the rich as far as their finances permitted. But the complicated dress and strict separation of the different strata of Edwardian society made it impossible for a poor person to wear the clothes of the rich. This extreme visual difference between rich and poor gradually modified with the rise of the middle classes. But World War II uniforms and

rationing destroyed and altered these visual signals so dramatically that it was not possible to tell the class of a woman by her clothes, only by the way she wore them. This was a bombshell landing plumb on one of the highest fences that divided the classes at the time, and its repercussions were felt all through the last century.

The work clothes of many Edwardian women differed little from those of her Victorian mother. Women working in service would have worn uniforms that can be suggested with aprons and caps over quite basic costume. The correct length of skirt – ankle-, knee- or calf-length – and the silhouette of the body, will point the period. The type of work a woman does will suggest the appropriate costume if you remember the difficulty of keeping clean. What sort of apron or over-sleeves will keep flour off your dress when baking? How would you tie the shawl that was keeping you warm in order to keep it out of the way when you were pulling carrots in a muddy field? What would you do with your baby if you had your hands full of baskets on your way to market? Aprons and overalls in a great variety of shapes and sizes can be copied from photographs of life at the time.

Accessories

These include hats, parasols, gloves, small bags, shoes, jewellery, and the belt and its variety of positions on the body.

> Two girls discuss evening dresses in the early 1930s: 'How lovely – green and silver velvet ... mine's silver lamé; it smells like a birdcage when it gets hot, but I do love it. Aren't you thankful evening dresses are long again?' (Nancy Mitford, *Love in a Cold Climate* published by Hamish Hamilton 1949)

> A young man in a beautifully cut suit of grey flannel was standing in the doorway. He had a long, vacant face topped by shining hair brushed back and heavily brilliantined after the prevailing mode ... (P. G. Wodehouse, 1923, Penguin Books)

Clothes for Men
Heads and Headgear

Hair: Moustaches were much in evidence at the beginning of the century. Hair was shortish, but not close-cropped, and in the twenties and thirties was being greased back by the fashionable man. Partings were straight and precise, and the tousled head was the mark of a country bumpkin or an artist.

Hair was worn shorter after the advent of war, and in fact the 'short-back-and-sides' and neat parting prevailed until well after World War II. A man with money would have had his hair cut by a professional barber, but many poorer heads would have been cut by the wife in the kitchen.

Hats: If you saw someone out without a hat you would wonder why, as you might if you saw a gentleman about without gloves and a walking stick. Most people of all classes wore them, and it is a most significant pointer to the past. A crowd of men in cloth caps, and a crowd of bareheaded men, will lead the audience to imagine totally different eras even if the rest of their clothes are identical.

The top hat: Top hats were worn with evening dress, and in the daytime. It is sometimes possible to buy them cheaply from places that supply uniforms for doormen. They are often grey, though these can be dyed or painted. Also, party and novelty shops sell versions of top hats. However, no efforts you make can provide a realistic substitute for the shiny, crisp

Men in the first half of the twentieth century.

outline of the real thing, and it is worth surmounting many difficulties to find one, because the message of status, period and class they give to an audience is utterly recognizable.

The bowler: Much worn in both town and country in the daytime. The same difficulties and solutions apply as to top hats.

The trilby. A felt hat with a fairly generous brim and a dented top, worn in the country and later in town. They could be brown, black or grey, but were never coloured.

The straw hat. Panamas and boaters were both worn in the summer in the country, and can be found in the same style in shops today.

The cap. The tweed cloth cap was worn by all classes for casual or sporting occasions, and by working men most of the time. It is not easy today to find cloth caps of the exact shape and fullness of the past, but the general impression that a modern one will give to most of the audience is still valuable.

Clothing the Body
Shirts and collars: Collars and shirt cuffs at this time had an importance they do not have today. It is hard for us to imagine, in these days of easy-care fabrics and washing machines, the exhausting difficulty of doing the washing when most houses had no running water. Starched collars and sometimes cuffs were attached to the shirts with studs, and it was quite usual to put a fresh collar on a dirty shirt. White, starched linen told the world that you were a solvent man doing a clean job. Those who worked in less genteel circumstances took the detachable collars, sometimes made of paper or thin card to save laundry, off their shirts. Collars and top pockets can be removed from modern shirts to clothe the working man, and the collars of modern shirts can be reshaped to resemble the outline of the variously shaped collars that would have been in fashion for the period.

Waistcoats: It was as usual for men and older boys to wear waistcoats in those days, as it is for them to wear sweaters today. They could match the jacket and trousers, or be in a contrasting fabric. Working men removed their jackets and collars, rolled up their sleeves and worked in their waistcoats and trousers. A gentleman wore his jacket over his waistcoat in the presence of ladies unless engaged in sporting or very informal pursuits. Waistcoats are a great boon to the costumier on a low budget as they are easy to make and alter, they give suits a more period look, and they hide the fact that the top of the trousers may look more modern than they should. They can also be decorative and flattering.

Suits, jackets and trousers: Men's clothes throughout the first half of the century retained a formality, and this is the feature to latch on to if your budget will not stretch to hiring the correct suits and accessories of the time, or the production does not need accurate costume. Tweed or light linen suits could be worn in the country, but dark suits were worn in the city. The morning coats and tailcoats that are still worn today for special occasions can be used; modern suits can be altered to give a closer impression of the past.

Early in the century men wore trousers with a front and a back crease, the legs narrowed at the bottom and occasionally had a turn-up. As the century moved on to the 1920s, turn-ups became the usual addition to the wider hem of the trouser legs, and they were to remain fashionable until after World War II. Trousers were cut to be worn with braces, and a belted pair was a clumsy affair of working convenience. If the only available outfit is a

A typical workman. Note the shirt worn without its detachable collar, also the waistcoat, cap and apron.

Ties: It was rare for a man not to wear a tie unless he engaged in very rough work. The styles and colours of this accessory changed regularly, and are easy to recreate from today's ties. The changes may be slight (a larger or smaller knot, bright polka dots or a discrete stripe), but they were one of the few outlets for man to make a bold statement with his dress. Black bow ties and waistcoats were worn with dinner jackets, and white bow ties and white waistcoats with the stiff-fronted shirt that went with evening tails.

Work Clothes
Working-class male costume retained the three-piece formality of coat, trousers and waistcoat. The coat might be taken off and the shirtsleeves rolled up, but often the waistcoat would stay on even under an apron or overall. There was still a feeling that it was a little unseemly to show your braces to a lady. A clear way to show the difference in class is by the sleek or crumpled outline, the polished or dusty shoe, the groomed or ruffled hair, and the consciousness on the part of the designer as to how much time and money a man has to spend on his appearance and the situation in which he works. The clothes of the clerk in an office would not be suitable for the gamekeeper who must work outside in all weathers.

Accessories
Hats, gloves, walking sticks, watch-chains, a handkerchief in the breast jacket pocket, ties and cravats.

Clothes for Children
Children, both rich and poor, of the first half of the nineteenth century wore hats out-of-doors. They were usually simpler versions of adult hats, and can be recreated from modern sources. For the first two decades of the nineteenth century sailor suits were popular for little boys and, with skirts, for little girls.

modern suit, make every possible effort to make collar, tie, waistcoat and shoes, along with hat, stick, gloves and hairstyle, give the right message. Men are less inclined to adopt the extremes of fashion than women, and the suit has changed much less than women's dresses during the twentieth century.

Knitted sweaters or jerseys: Sweaters were worn from around the second decade of the century, but only for sporting or very informal occasions. Sleeveless sweaters, knitted cardigans and jerseys were close-fitting, and could be coloured or patterned.

Useful ideas.

Pinafores and sailor collars, waistcoats, and trousers cut off into long shorts or breeches and the correct silhouette will give an impression of the formality of the past. There is something about calf-length thin socks without turnovers, with just-below-knee length skirts or breeches and a hat, which sets a child in this era even if the costume is not historically correct.

In the later years of the period children's clothes simplified. Boys wore shorts and knee socks until puberty, and many for some time afterwards. The transition from short to long trousers remained a moment of excitement and importance for boys until the 1950s. Girls wore jerseys and pleated skirts or smocked dresses unless they were dressed up in frills for a special occasion.

Accessories
Hats, sailor collars, hair ribbons for girls, socks, toys.

9 A World in the Living Room 1945–2000

The Life of the Time and its Clothes

In 1947 Christian Dior swirled metres of skirt round a model, nipped in her waist, crowned her with a romantic hat and sent her image out to women as the New Look. Women, hungry for the opportunity to play with their femininity after the strictures of rationing, were delighted. Men's clothes relaxed as they were freed, yet again, from the rules of uniform. The Festival of Britain, followed by the coronation of a second Queen Elizabeth, affirmed the promise of peace, plenty and optimism to post-war Britain, and gave people a chance to celebrate the settled mood.

The children, in those convalescent years of the fifties, grew up and became the spearhead of the amazing parade of fashion that has been with us ever since. Television and the wireless, as well as newspapers and magazines, brought the world into the sitting room of many households. The family unit, contained in the larger units of its locality, began to push out its walls. The teenagers of the 1960s began the series of quick-fire changes accompanied by the urgent excitement of rock-and-roll. Fashion galloped. Teddy boys, mods, rockers, beatniks, hippies, hell's angels, punks, goths and all, began their fantastic parade on the streets of Britain. These extremes of fashion, each accompanied by its signature tunes, belonged to small groups of young people who wanted to demonstrate their separation from the lives and values of their parents – less rebellious teenagers dressed like their mothers and fathers.

A teenage boy in late 1950 wears an outfit calculated to enrage the older generation: '... the grey pointed alligator casuals [shoes], the pink neon pair of ankle crêpe nylon- stretch [socks], my Cambridge blue glove-fit jeans, a vertical-striped happy shirt revealing my lucky neck-charm on its chain, and the Roman-cut short-arse jacket ... not to mention my wrist identity jewel and my Spartan warrior hair-do ...'. (From *Absolute Beginners* by Colin MacInnes, published MacGibbon & Kee, 1960)

The excitement and availability of high street fashion and the great numbers of the teenagers and twenty-year-olds who wore it, meant that it was impossible to tell the class of young people by the clothes they wore. This may sound unimportant now, but it was one of the major hammers that began bashing away at the walls that had existed between classes before World War II. Another was the transistor radio. The single wireless in the sitting room listened to by the whole family was supplemented by a radio that was cheap enough to be owned by many teenagers. Young people of all classes sung, danced, made love and despaired to the same songs. And they bought the same records as soon as they could afford a record player.

Most men and women in their early twenties and their children, whose clothes were chosen for them, dressed in more conventional ways. Men went to the office in a suit, white shirt and tie that differed little from that of a time before the war. Women, as ever more open to fashion changes, followed the lead given by Paris and bought ready-made and more practical versions of catwalk fashions in the high street. But some, particularly older women, or those who lived away from urban centres and influences, still wore the below-

calf-length skirts and undistinguished cut of clothes of thirty years before.

There are factors that separate this period from any other in history. The most influential for the stage designer, if not for the historian, is that it falls within the living memory of many members of today's audience. Times that seem so far away to those born towards the end of the century are clear and close to those who lived through them. Consequently the swings of fashion, so ephemeral and changing, have to have a particular reality if they are to convince. Women who remember putting on stockings will remember what the stockings looked and felt like, and how they kept them up. Many of these memories are of life within a confined social circle, and detailed research is necessary to pinpoint the differences between men and women in different areas, classes and jobs.

Photographs of fashion models, who are visually a race apart, or actors in films, who are wearing clothes chosen by a costume designer, give an inaccurate and often bizarre picture of the past. However, the clothes and behaviour of ordinary people going about their daily business can be seen in photographs and documentaries produced at the time. People of today are familiar with the idea of fashion flitting in and out of their lives with different force at different times and ages. These records also show us the ages and groups of people who wore the latest fashions in the past, and display a more standardized style than might be expected, given the range and invention of clothes available.

Violent changes in social behaviour, urban life and fashion occurred in the 1960s and 1970s, and the pendulum of fashion swung wildly between the past, which seemed secure in the distance of time, and the exciting space-age future. The longing for a fictionally romantic past where the lumps and bumps were ironed out by time, and a push towards a minimalist future where geometry organized the chaos of change, continued to influence the arts, architecture and fashion throughout the rest of the century. The pleasure of dressing up – never far from human hearts – was reflected in the clothes then, and continues to reappear in clothes today. In one shop a young man, no longer obliged to dress up in the uniform of National Service, might have bought the black leather, silver-studded, zipped and brutalized concoction redolent of past or future fictional battles. His girlfriend, freed from the pressure of marriage as the only career, might have glued her hair into the threatening spikes of a marauding mercenary. In the shop next door her sister could be trying on the pastel print, lace-collared reproduction of a demure nineteenth-century woman, and her brother hiring a dress suit and bow tie much like his father's and grandfather's for a college ball.

In the 1980s women demonstrated their new equality in the clothes they wore to work, though the broad shoulders that suggested the male silhouette were often countermanded by the femininity of the skirt. Women in professional jobs began to wear trousers at work. Casual clothes could be alike for both sexes. Two women ruled the country, the Queen on the throne and the first female Prime Minister in Parliament. They both chose to wear that particular badge of British respectability: the jacket and skirt and handbag, and their well documented appearances in these suits provide a lesson to the costume designer. The small differences in colour, cut, accessories and deportment clearly define the characters of the two women, and demonstrate how little is required to give the audience an understanding of the people they see onstage.

Women, though still fighting for greater parity, had achieved equality unimaginable in the previous century, and their clothes reflected this change. Perhaps the strongest outward sign of this victory was not the trouser suit, the briefcase or the barrister's wig, but the jeans, and the confident walk that went with them. By the 1960s there was a pair in most teenage wardrobes. They spread through age, sex and class. Today there can be few British men, women or children born after World War II who do not own a pair of jeans. The message they give – whether on a princess or a builder, in a palace or a pub – is dictated by the shape, the accessories and the occasion. It is remarkable that jeans and a T-shirt, the closest we come to a class-less uniform, are subject to such exacting and recognizable differences of cut and quality. Previously only a few people who were used to looking at expensive clothes could recognize the exclusive cut of a Savile Row suit or a Dior dress; but at the end of the twentieth century the logos of the designer blazoned on the clothes trumpeted their cost, and an attendant assumption of their quality, in a way that was recognizable even to children.

Extraordinary events, things unimaginable at the beginning of the century, had happened with great rapidity. Who could have believed that men would walk on the moon, that ordinary people could fly through the sky to the other side of the world, or sit at home and flash information all round the world. That solvent and educated men and women could walk about half naked from choice, or that paupers could die of cold outside a shop window full of light, warmth and furs, and excite less comment than the result of a game. Or that millions of people could be slaughtered by an adversary they could not see, and a broken human heart could be made to work again.

The huge range of fashion that could be seen walking across one zebra crossing in the second half of the twentieth century was phenomenal. The clothes that people wore could give out the most accurate visual

Trendy academics in 1975: 'Howard ... has long hair and a Zapata moustache; he wears neat white sweatshirts, with rousing symbols on the front, like clenched fists, and hairy loose waistcoats, and pyjama-style blue jeans. Barbara, who is big and has frizzled yellow hair, wears green eyeshadow, and clown-white make-up, and long caftan dresses, and no bra ...' (From *The History Man* by Malcolm Bradbury, published in 1975)

message to anyone who saw them: signs of the circle in which they moved, their financial situation, their interests and their allegiances.

It is difficult to see the years of this half-century, so close to our own, as history. To us, today, they appear as jangled and separate images. We can't dance to the rhythm of the whole time, only to the disjointed phrases we catch as they rush by us. The speed with which these images and sounds succeed each other, and the ease with which we can view and hear them with so little physical and intellectual effort, encourages the fragmentation of our understanding. We have to wait until the distance of time makes us able to focus on the whole picture.

CREATING THE CLOTHES OF THE TIME FOR THE STAGE

Clothes for Women

Heads and Headgear

Hair: The head in the first decade of this period was small, neat and carefully arranged. If hair was long it was worn up in a French pleat or a flattened bun that did not disturb the line of the neck and hat. In the 1960s hairdressers, who had begun to occupy a more important place in the fashion industry, began to invent styles to complement the rushing flood of invention. It is overcomplicated to try and chart the journey of hairstyles as the changes are so many, so fleeting and sometimes so extraordinary. By the end of the century hair had once again become a 'crowning glory' to many women, though some cropped theirs close or even shaved their heads. Advertisements urged the purchase of miraculous products to promote and colour glossy, beautiful hair with the same vigour as Edwardian mothers urged their daughters to brush it a hundred times to produce the same result. It became acceptable to dye hair. Despite a variety of opportunities for change, less fashion-conscious women kept to an unremarkable style or one very like the one they had worn in their youth.

Make-up: Make-up followed hair and clothes in its variety, and settled towards the end of the century to a natural look. The subtle use of cosmetics was for effect and not to hide the fact that they were being used. No stigma at all was attached to a woman's attempts to enhance her beauty with make-up. Wealthy women unsatisfied with their appearances bought facelifts and other surgical procedures in attempts to improve things, and these created the same frisson of interest, speculation and occasional disapproval that was accorded to make-up in past centuries.

Hats: The hats of the period are many and various, but after 1950 are worn more for fun and warmth than respectability. There are a

Two girls, in extremes of young fashion, out shopping in 1980: 'Their hair was teased up into tormented pineapples of orange and green fluff, their potentially supple young limbs trapped and strapped into what appeared to be plastic armour'. (*Love's Labours* by Sue Limb, published by Corgi in 1989)

Women in the second half of the twentieth century.

few occasions still, such as weddings and royal functions, when women are expected to wear hats. All the hats of the time can be recreated from those available for sale today.

Caps: The peaked cap has had several revivals in this period. First, as the civilian version of a uniform hat in the late forties; then as a full-crowned cap with the mini-skirt of the 1960s; and finally, in coloured cotton often embossed with a logo, on men, young women and children, with all sorts of casual clothes and sportswear.

Legs and Feet
The arrival of seamless stockings freed women from always having to make sure the seams ran straight up the back of the leg. Tights, which were produced to wear with the short skirts of the 1960s, got rid of the uncomfortable and lumpy suspenders, which held up the stockings. Ankle, knee and overknee socks, leg warmers and leggings all made brief appearances; but tights – whether sheer, opaque, woolly, coloured or patterned – remain the most popular for wearing with skirts. Court shoes with low or high heels have kept their popularity with more formal clothes, but shoes or boots of all kinds, and above all, trainers, can be seen on feet in any street. The correct shoes will help an audience recognize characters from each era within this period, and will also help the actors with the walk that goes with the clothes.

Clothing the Body
Dresses: It is difficult to follow the fantasies of fashion in this era. Magazines, films, television and advertisements have made us all familiar with the look of the latest fashion – though the extremes of imagination on the catwalk are displayed on models whose bodies, make-up and gait have little to do with most of our lives. The clothes worn by nearly all women are influenced by this parade, but in many cases the influence is subtle. Skirt length and the silhouette of clothes, shoes and hairstyle appear on the High Street in a less exaggerated form. Each new invention is echoed in a more restrained style by the clothes of those who assume they are not influenced by current fashion. The silhouette changed with the new look with its wasp waist and full skirt, and then the elegant pencil skirt, the thigh-high mini-skirt and the ankle-length maxi skirt, the casual separates, the broad-shouldered tight-skirted suits, the romantic frills and the little slip dresses. The styles, so exciting in their season, seep into the consciousness of women and a skirt suddenly looks too long, or ridiculously short. A woman may still, in the second millennium, wear a shirt-waisted dress much the same shape as the one she wore in 1950; there will usually be slight differences in outline and length that will make it look as if it belongs to today, rather than the past. Most men and women have an instinctive ability to adjust to the fashion of the day without aping extremes.

Clothes and dress patterns from this era can be found in second-hand shops, and the pictorial reference is readily available. As always, it is most important to remember how few women dress in the height of fashion, and to look at real people on streets or in documentaries.

> Different styles prevailed for young women in the late 1950s: 'Caroline's friends padded around in tight stretch trousers and ballet slippers. Francesca put on her luncheon dress, a navy poplin with too much gathered skirt to be severe and no white pique, which she thought made her look secretarial. She ... bought a plain, schoolgirlish brimmed hat, ... a fawn hat, ...' (*Still Life* by A. S. Byatt, published by Chatto and Windus 1985)

Trousers: A photograph of a market place in 1950 would show many women in hats, most carrying baskets, and few women in trousers. A photograph of the same scene fifty years later would show few women in hats, most women carrying plastic carrier bags, and the majority of women in trousers. By 1970, trousers, and particularly the trouser suit, were beginning to be acceptable wear for most occasions, and by the end of the century the occasions that demanded a skirt were few. Smart trousers, worn with court shoes and blouse rather than T-shirt and trainers, had become acceptable. Despite this there still remained in the last decade of the century a feeling, in unsophisticated, old-fashioned or determinedly traditional circles, that trousers were not suitable formal wear for a woman.

Work Clothes

The great choice and cheapness of ready-made clothes made the same fashions available to all, though the quality of cloth and cut differed. Coloured tabards and overalls replaced aprons for work that demanded them, but much protective clothing became unnecessary, as street clothes were as easy to wash as aprons. The accessories, the grooming and the deportment of a character can give a clearer message to the audience about the character than the costume.

Accessories

Gloves, hats, bags, jewellery, scarves, dark glasses, umbrellas, briefcases, polythene shopping bags and mobile phones.

Clothes for Men

Hair: The style of short back and sides and neat parting was retained after the war. Indeed, some men kept it throughout their lives, but younger men began to grow their hair, and by the 1960s it very often curled on the collar. Sideboards, beards and hair greased into a quiff over the forehead were worn by young men. Hippies grew their hair very long, and after a gap of 300 years, men appeared once again on London's streets with luxuriant, curling heads of hair. This vogue for very long hair, although retained by a few men who mostly worked in the arts, died out and by the 1970s it was short once again. The 1990s brought with it a fashion for very short crew cuts, or even shaved heads, which gained in popularity throughout the last decade of the century.

Hats: Bowlers or trilbies were worn at the beginning of the period. The bowler continued to be worn by traditional city businessmen, but after the mid-1960s, hats of many different shapes were worn only for fun or warmth, and the etiquette which had governed the wearing of hats died out. Hats have been retained as part of many uniforms, perhaps because they create such a recognisable silhouette.

Caps. The tweed, peaked cap was worn by working men and sportsmen throughout the period. The cotton peaked cap, a cousin of the American baseball cap, was worn with casual dress by most young men of the nineties.

Feet and Footware

The conventional lightweight lace-up walking shoe remained a staple fashion. Other shoes, boots, sandals and, of course, the trainer have accompanied it at various times on its path through the century. The daily task of shoe polishing, which was a feature of so many mornings in the 1950s and early 1960s, has become a more unusual activity. Trainers were worn with casual clothes as well as for sporting activity. Socks of all kinds, colours and patterns were worn, though dark socks are more usual with a conventional formal shoe.

Men in the second half of the twentieth century.

Clothing the Body

Suits. The dark two- or three-piece suit still existed as the base note of formal fashion, and changed remarkably little in fifty years. The lapels and trouser widths help to set the suit in its period. The tie, shirt and hairstyle will point the era more clearly to the audience than the cut of the suit. More imaginatively designed suits appeared at various times, but they were adopted by a few men for a short time and had little effect on the traditional image. Central heating, however, had a noticeable effect on the weight of cloth used, and the suits of the end of the century were much lighter in weight than those of the 1950s.

Casual clothes: The places and occasions where it became acceptable to wear casual clothes marked as great a revolution in its way as any change in the actual fashions. At the beginning of the period most men wore ties and jackets outside their own homes and gardens, and there was a difference in the clothes that men wore for informal occasions and the clothes they wore for sport. Chains of high-street shops began to sell fashionable clothes at a reasonable price. The ease with which clothes can be washed, and the fact that people of all classes can afford them, have helped to relax the attitudes and dress codes of society. Sweaters, previously worn in the same way as a waistcoat, or for sporting activities, began to be worn outside the home, at first as a V-neck with a collar and tie, then with less formal accessories. By the end of the century the sweater or sweatshirt and the T-shirt could be seen more often than the suit on any street outside the city. Summer in the city at the beginning of the period would have seen nearly all the men in long sleeves and jackets, and certainly long trousers. A summer weekend in the city in 2000 would be a sea of bare legs and arms.

The jacket: The garment known as a sports jacket or sports coat at the beginning of the period was cut like a formal suit jacket and made of tweed, flannel or linen. It was an alternative to the suit for informal wear, and was worn with shirt and tie, or with a cravat and an open-necked shirt on extremely relaxed occasions. Various alternatives – from the mid-thigh draped version of the teddy boy, to the waist-length bomber jacket, and the hooded anorak in all colours, cloths and leathers – began to be worn. But the sports jacket hung on, and still hangs on today in the wardrobes of older or more conservative men.

Casual trousers: In twill, corduroy, wool, cotton and many washable fabrics, these followed the line of suit trousers – but the success story of the century was jeans. Jeans arrived in England from America in the 1950s and became the most popular and most widely worn informal garment of the period. This informality did not prevent the influence of fashion on their shape. Teenagers have swum in their jeans to shrink them to a figure-hugging second skin, they have sewn triangular gussets in the side seam to widen the hems, have ripped and patched, bleached and embroidered, and chased the slight changes in the design of this strong, denim pair of trousers. Jeans – tight and baggy, designer fashionable or work-worn practical – were everywhere, and still are. By the end of the century most men owned a pair of jeans.

The shirt: The shirt made remarkable changes in this era, the most dramatic being its translation to a coloured and fashionable outer garment. In 1947 most men wore white shirts with a collar and tie. It was acceptable, in an informal situation, to take off the jacket and tie, undo the top button and roll up the sleeves – but this process would be reversed if a bow needed to be made to respectability. Subtle checks or stripes, particularly on warm winter shirts, or short-sleeved ones, were for manual workers or casual wear. Dark-coloured shirts, perhaps worn with a contrasting bow tie, were a sign of artistic or bohemian leanings. Collars – long-pointed, rounded and mandarin – made appearances. Some shirts had just the neckband and no collar at all. Shapes were full, fitted, cut with yokes or without, and wide or narrow sleeves according to the silhouette in fashion at the time. Shirts became as varied and as subject to fashion as women's dresses. Young men at first, and then some older men when dressed informally, wore their shirts outside their trousers. Despite this explosion of change, those men who wore a suit to work wore it with a long-sleeved shirt buttoned to the neck and tucked in the trousers, and with a tie.

The informal short sleeves and jersey shirt with a collar or a polo neck – all of which were occasionally worn with a degree of panache instead of a shirt and tie under a suit – ushered in the T-shirt, a simple, washable, comfortable and adaptable garment which, by the end of the century, was worn as a top garment, an under-vest, a shirt or a pyjama top. But despite all this excitement, the crisp, perfectly laundered white shirt never lost its place in formal dress.

> Casual clothes and smart clothes: '... the creaseless grey flannels and aged corduroy jacket which he wore day in day out ...' were exchanged, in the evening, for his 'one decent suit, one clean white shirt, and one smart tie, all of which, together with polished shoes and a neatly shaved face, transformed him utterly'. (*The L-Shaped Room* by Lynne Reid Banks, published by Chatto and Windus 1960)

Ties: Ties varied in shape from the bootlace tie that was little more than a cord and a toggle, to the wide kipper tie; they were made in cotton, silk and man-made fibres in all colours and particularly patterns. A tie specially designed for a particular school, club or regiment was a feature of men's dress throughout the century, and a way of recognizing a fellow student or club member, as heraldic devices had been in the past. But the wearing of a tie gradually declined, and by the turn of the century it was only worn in professions that required a traditional standard of dress or in formal circumstances.

Work Clothes

All work clothes became less specific throughout the period. It was more acceptable for those engaged in dirty manual work to travel in their work clothes, and there were fewer stigmas attached to not looking smart. Thus in 1950 a gardener might go to work in jacket, waistcoat and perhaps even a tie, and on arrival take off the jacket and tie, roll up his shirt sleeves, and put on an apron. Now he would travel to work in the easily washable and classless T-shirt, sweater and jeans, which constituted his work clothes. All clothes, except the most formal and expensive, are now found as 'work clothes': the choice depends on the sort of work, and the quality depends on the income of the wearer and the importance they attach to their image.

Accessories

Ties, casual hats, scarves, mobile phones, briefcases, sports-type bags and rucksacks.

Clothes for Children

Children's clothes throughout the period became more comfortable and easy to wash. For a decade or so after the war, boys wore jackets or blazers, and shirts and ties like their fathers, for school or for those occasions that called for best clothes; girls wore skirts or

dresses. Young children's clothes continued to reflect the taste of their parents, but the age at which children followed fashion became younger as their exposure to the world shown on television increased. By the end of the century there was scarcely any difference except in size in the play or off-duty clothes of the parents and the play clothes of their children. Once again, children dressed as little adults, but more comfortably than ever before. The advent of cotton jersey, which replaced so much of the woven cotton, made clothes easier to wear and care for. Trousers for girls became acceptable at all occasions, including school. In a strange reversal which illustrates the vagaries of fashion, shorts, now they were no longer compulsory for young boys, ceased to be a despised symbol of childhood and were worn for choice by adolescent boys, though these were often forbidden as school wear. It is probably only a matter of time before it will be a rebellious act for a girl to wear a skirt to school.

When dressing children of this very varied and recognizable time for the stage, it is the hair, the shoes and the socks or tights that help to set the characters in their time. The concept of 'Sunday best' has vanished today, but it still existed throughout much of the nineteenth century.

10 PATTERNS, MODIFICATIONS AND SUBSTITUTIONS

The patterns in this section can be subjected to endless modifications of size and shape, since their exact measurement depends on that of the actor. Actual measurements have only been given for extra clarification, and they can be altered at will by the cutter. The more complex shapes, such as the coif and the corset, could be enlarged on a photocopier.

HEADS AND HEADGEAR

Hair

It is always better to style an actor's own hair than to use a wig unless you can afford a good one. Good wigs are expensive, and cheap ones look unconvincing. Try to persuade your cast to grow or cut their hair in a way suitable for their role. Hairdressers will sometimes give professional help and advice in exchange for an advertisement in the programme. Hair gel, oil or wax, curling tongs, false buns, hairpieces and colour sprays should be used in conjunction with nets and hair ornaments to create a look of the period. Fine hairnets, which do not show onstage, help keep a style neat during the rigors of performance. Among the many hair accessories is a sort of gritty doughnut, which helps create a secure bun when the hair is not really long enough. Different ethnic groups use different accessories, all of which can be useful for stage hair styling, and it is worth scouring markets in all sorts of different areas to find out what is available.

If you want actors to wear a beard, sideboards or a moustache, give them as much warning as possible so they can grow their own if they prefer. Carefully groomed hair, untidy hair, and the strictness or casualness of the style, say a great deal about character with the flick of a comb. Imagine the same head with neatly slicked back hair and a monocle; or a floppy, untidy fringe and round spectacles; or a shaved head and dark glasses.

Make-Up

Street make-up tends to be used more than traditional stage make-up today, unless a particular effect is required. The distance from which the audience view the actor should be considered, and the finished effect checked from the front and back of the audience when the stage lights are on. It takes a great deal of experience before an actor can tell in the dressing room what the make-up will look like onstage. A style of make-up, naturalistic or otherwise, which is appropriate to the style of production should be decided in consultation with designer and cast.

Hats

Modern hats that can be found second-hand, can be adapted to make styles from the past if

A variety of hats.

there is not enough money to buy professional equipment and supplies from a millinery supplier.

Felt Hats
These can have their brims cut off, or they can be trimmed or added to. The brim can be glued or stitched up in different places to change the shape. Felt hats can be stretched by holding them over a steaming kettle and stretching the crown with the fingers.

Straw Hats
These can have the shape of their brims altered by drawing the new shape on the hat with a pencil, zigzagging just inside the line, trimming off the excess, and binding or re-zigzagging the resulting raw edge. If you try to cut the hat before you stitch it, it will fray and may collapse.

The Hood
A triangular shape that can be cut with or without a point to lie close to the head like chain mail, or flop to the shoulders like a monk's hood.

The Tube Hat
A most adaptable shape, very like the pull-on knitted hats of today. Make a 75cm (30in) long tube of stretchy cloth, cotton or woollen type jersey, which widens at the bottom to about 80cm (32in) in circumference, or experiment with the sleeve of an old sweater. Roll the wide end up over a circle of wadding until it fits snugly on the head. You will see how easily this shape can be adapted for rich and poor by altering the length of the tube and the decoration of the padded roll.

Top Hats, Puritan-Type Hats, Bowlers
When money is short, structured men's hats can present a problem. Party, novelty and fancy-dress shops sell pressed felt and cardboard hats in different traditional styles; these look too lightweight to be convincing, but they can be used as a base and given more body with a covering of felt, cloth, papier mâché or paint.

Skull Caps
These can be cut from the crown of any felt hat. They can be round, or shaped over the

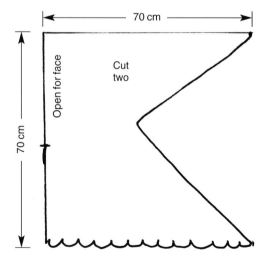

Hood.

Component parts of a Puritan hat.

ears. The best way to get a perfect fit if you haven't got a hat block is to hold the cap over a steaming kettle, then let it dry whilst it is being smoothed to the head that is going to wear it. However, not every actor is delighted by this infallible but unorthodox method, which requires more charm than skill.

Women's Caps
The cap has been worn in many different forms throughout the centuries. Three basic methods that can be adapted for most caps, wimples and coifs are given overleaf.

Men's Caps
Peaked caps can be made of a circular or oval piece of cloth gathered into a band, or of several more or less triangular sections, which produce a more fitted shape. The size and shape of the peak and the importance or otherwise of the band vary, but the basic shape and construction can be copied from today's caps. Alterations to the pattern can be made to increase or reduce the size of the crown. The cotton versions with an adjustable back fastening, which have grown out of the American baseball cap, are a symbol of the late twentieth century, but with the brims cut off they can form a secure foundation for many period headdresses.

The Beret
Use a circle of cloth, dustbin-lid size, for a big, floppy Tudor hat; or dinner-plate size for a neat 1940s one, gathered into a band to fit the head.

Crowns and Coronets
Illustrations of different shapes are easy to find, and they can be recreated in many different materials. Stiffened cloth, painted foam, various plastics and felting can look more convincing and be more practical to wear than a more authentic re-creation of metal. An apparent weight can be suggested by thickening the edges to make the whole object appear heavier than it is. Crowns must look convincingly heavy if they are to be believable.

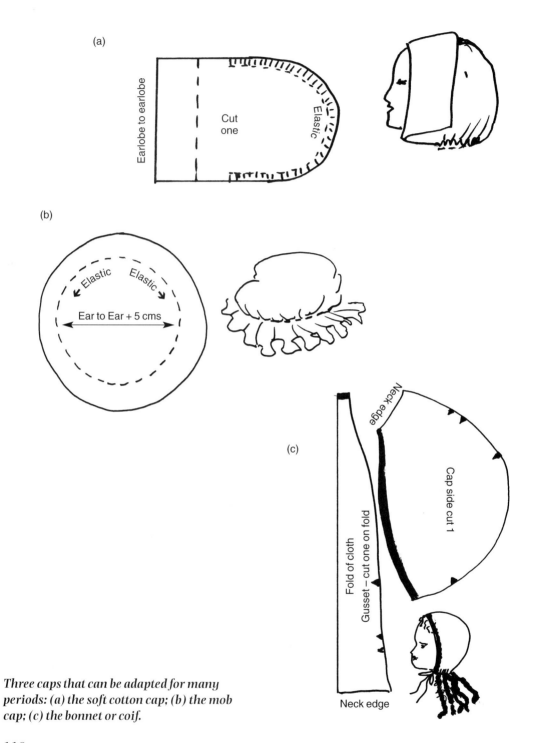

Three caps that can be adapted for many periods: (a) the soft cotton cap; (b) the mob cap; (c) the bonnet or coif.

A strip of foam round the inside will make them cling to the head and avoid the disastrous theatrical gaff of a crown falling off at the wrong time.

Legwear

Stockings and Tights

Stockings for men or women can be kept up with a suspender belt or garters above or below the knee. If you have to let out a suspender belt for a man, do it at the sides or the suspenders will end up in the wrong place. Tights stay up better on men when worn with elastic braces. Long socks or stockings can be bought from shops or markets that serve a wide ethnic mix of customers. They can be dyed easily, particularly if they have a good proportion of cotton in their fibre – the more cotton, the richer the colour. Seamed stockings for women can be found in department stores but are often too thin and may need to be worn over a pair of tights. In World War II, women drew lines up the backs of their legs to imitate seamed stockings when they were not available, and there is nothing to stop you doing the same and wearing a pair of modern tights over the top. Tights for men can be made like long tubular leggings if the cloth has a good two-way elastic stretch. Less stretchy cloth requires more careful shaping and measuring of foot and leg.

Cut the foot pattern from a pair of socks, and allow plenty of length in the leg. Men's tights can be bought from ballet suppliers and dyed. Leggings with a loop of elastic under the heel can be used instead of tights if the shoe hides the gap. Tubes of cloth, like leg warmers, worn over tights can be used when a thick, wrinkled look is wanted. The smooth line of neat stockings or tights, and the wrinkled and unflattering bagginess when they sag round legs and ankles, are useful signs of character.

Shoes

No historical costume can give a convincing picture unless the shoes are considered as part of the whole. The footwear worn by an actor influences the way he moves, and even today the shoes we wear govern our gait. It is possible, though expensive, to buy copies of past styles from specialist suppliers. Dance, martial art, sporting outfitters and wedding shops stock shoes outside the normal range of the high street. Modern shoes can be adapted.

Search for a shape that is close to the style of the time. Check that the soles are not too heavy – thick rubber soles look unconvincing on period feet. Shoes can be dyed with shoe dye, or painted with several thin coats of spray paint. They can be covered with fabric and be decorated as appropriate. It is useful to know that if you slice a lace-up on either side of the tongue, the shoe can be laced beneath the tongue and this produces a good base for many period shoes. The tops of shoes or short boots can be re-cut to a new shape, and tops or gaiters can be added to make them into boots. An ankle boot provides ample opportunity for re-cutting into a period shoe, and has the advantage of leaving you with matching scraps for straps or other decoration.

An interested and enthusiastic shoemaker or mender can make more complicated alterations with his specialist machinery if you can manage to explain exactly what you want. Instructions have to be clear and precise, and often results as good can be achieved with a sturdy pair of scissors, a hole punch and determination; a leather needle can be fitted in the machine if you need to stitch the shoe. Trainers belong to the present and the later decades of the last century. They produce a gait in men and women that destroys any effort a designer can make to create an impression of the past.

A pair of shoes. One has been re-cut and laced under the tongue.

CLOTHING THE BODY

Shirts and Blouses

Three basic shapes can be adapted to make tunics, shifts, shirts and blouses, which will prove useful for both sexes in many different periods. The size, fullness and length can all be altered according to the costume being made, but the basic patterns remain the same.

The Romantic Shirt

The pattern for this can be adapted from a modern man's shirt. Choose one with a yoke. The yoke should be widened at the shoulder so that the sleeves drop slightly over the upper arm. The sleeves should be cut with extra length and fullness, which is gathered into the armholes. Extra width in the back and front is gathered into the yoke. An alternative is to cut new wide sleeves for an existing shirt. Patterns for the tunic shirt and the full blouse are illustrated.

The Full Blouse

This should be made in a lightweight cloth such as muslin, and can be used as a blouse under a bodice or as a full-length shift.

The Tunic Shirt

This simple pattern could be cut long or short in sacking or in silk, and be frilled or patched according to the wealth of the wearer.

Altering Collars

The collar is often the only part of the shirt that shows, and it can be altered to suit the period. The collar on a standard man's shirt or woman's blouse can be cut off completely to leave a collar-band, or reshaped entirely by drawing the new shape on the old collar while it is still attached to the shirt, stitching round, cutting off the excess, and zigzagging with a close stitch. Alternatively the collar can be cut off and used as a pattern base for an enlarged

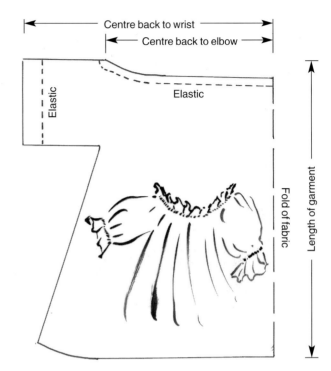

Centre back to wrist

Centre back to elbow

Elastic

Elastic

Fold of fabric

Length of garment

*The full blouse,
undershift
or smock.*

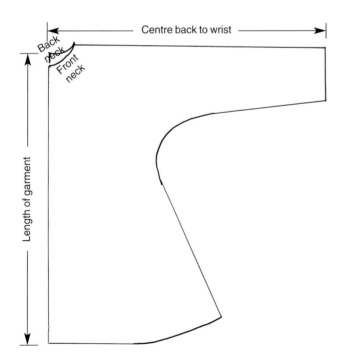

Centre back to wrist

Back neck

Front neck

Length of garment

The tunic shirt.

121

(a)

(b)

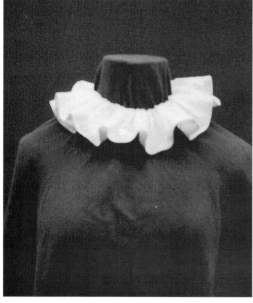

(c)

Three ruffs: (a) pleated, (b) gathered onto a band and (c) on elastic.

or completely different collar. A collar that matches the shirt can be cut from the shirt tails.

Ruffs

(a) **Pleated ruff:** Allow at least ten times the neck measurement for pleating. Close pleats on a wide neckband may use up to thirty times the neck measurement.
(b) **Gathered ruff:** Allow 5m (16ft 5in) for gathering into a narrow neckband, and stitch pleats every 20cm (8in) on the outside edge to keep them under control.
(c) **The ruffle.** Made like a 'scrunchy' from a 2m (6ft) tube of cotton gathered with elastic.

Bodices
The inexperienced sewer may find it easier to alter a ready-made blouse or lightweight jacket than to create one from scratch – at least the fastenings will be in place, and all that needs to be done is to fit the garment. Many modern blouses and shirts can, with careful fitting, alteration of collar or neckline, and perhaps a dip in the dye pot, be used as articles of an earlier period. Study the fit of the time and try to recreate it by pinning the garment to shape on the actor. The easiest shape to adapt for a close fit is one cut with a seam running from shoulder to hem over the bust, as well as seams at the side.

Big-Sleeved Blouse
New, full sleeves can be cut to turn a dress into a fitted blouse of an earlier period. The full sleeves and perhaps a new high collar can be cut from the cloth in the skirt of the dress.

Corsets

Corsets are difficult to make and take a long

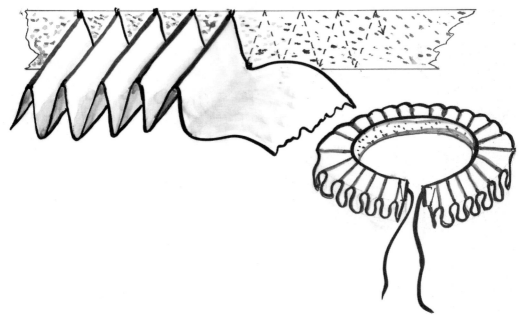

How to pleat a ruff.

CORSET

Lacing at the sides as well as the back makes adjustment on the body more variable. The corset is boned at centre front, centre back and sides.

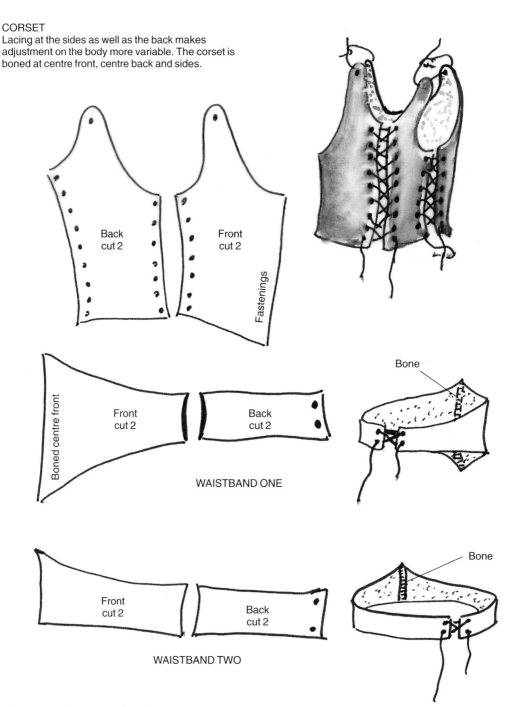

A corset and two waistbands.

time, but they are worth the trouble. Information on their correct construction can be found via the bibliography. The simplified pattern, and the two-boned waistbands illustrated in the diagrams, can be adapted to other styles, and will give a corseted shape and feeling to a basic costume. The corset can be boned and laced at the back, sides and shoulders to create a perfect fit. It can be worn alone, but would usually be used over a shift or blouse.

Skirts

The main difference between a modern skirt and a period skirt is in the length, and this is the first point to consider. The second is the fullness: in the past, the difference between rich and poor clothes was often in the quantity as well as the quality of the cloth used. The following patterns can be adapted for skirts of all periods, including those attached to dresses.

The Full Skirt

This is made from a length of cloth of appropriate length, gathered or pleated into a waistband. The hem can be 8m (26ft) or more around for a Victorian skirt, and long enough to be ground length when draped over a crinoline; or a metre (3ft) round the hem and 50cm (18in) long for a mini skirt. The method is the same, and any modern pattern can be adapted.

Flared Skirts

The principle of using a circle with a hole cut in the middle for the waist can be adapted for length: it gives fullness at the hem without bulk over the hips. The radius of the circle is the length plus ⅙ (one-sixth) of the waist measurement. The measurements can be adjusted so that the waist is wide enough to gather for extra fullness: in this case remember to allow extra length in the skirt.

Triangular Skirt

A shape that gives extra fullness at the back to allow for a train or a bustle.

Bum-Rolls, Bustles and Underskirts

Bum-rolls can be made from tubes of cloth or even a pair of tights stuffed with wadding; hip pads and bustles are like little cushions to tie round the waist. Both look better if they are shaped and tapered near the fastening tapes. Petticoats and underskirts should follow the shape of the top skirt, but can be made of any fabric of a suitable weight if they do not show. Their value is in the bulk they give to a skirt, or in making the top cloth slither over the skin. A simple crinoline effect can be created with a gathered knee-length petticoat with a hem width the same as the width of crinoline required. Boning cut 10cm (4in) longer than the hem threaded through a channel in the bottom will spring out to hold the circle rigid. The circle can be distorted to an oval shape with tapes at the side. A circle with a diameter of more than 60cm (24in) will need strong steel tape (available from well stocked haberdashery departments) if it is not to sag under the weight of the cloth.

Tabards

The most basic tabard is a length of cloth with a hole for the head, and it can be varied by splitting it down the front. This extremely simple shape, which can be any length or width, can be worn as a stiff, scarlet, gold-embroidered garment as worn by the royal trumpeters today; or, made in a ragged, dirty strip of wool, it can be appropriate for the mediaeval beggar. The cloth and its decoration are infinitely adaptable. It can be worn over a basic costume, and can give the impression of many different periods with the addition of a ruff, a wide lace collar, thick fur round the neck, or any significant accessory of the period.

125

CIRCLE SKIRT

The size of the inner circle controls the amount of gathers at the waist. The outer circle controls the length.

GATHERED SKIRT

The width controls the amount of fullness at the waist. It could be a little over a metre for a slim hipped skirt or over 10 metres for a victorian crinoline.

TRIANGLE SKIRT

The position and fullness of the gathers controls the shape of the skirt. It could be flat at the front with all the gathers at the back or equally full all the way round.

These three shapes, with adaptations of size, will make most period skirts.

BATTLEDRESS

Soldiers and their clothes and weapons present a problem to a designer working within a tight budget. However you design these costumes, the relative ranks of the soldiers must be apparent, as there are always leaders and followers in battle. Also, the uniforms of the last century may be recognizable to many of the audience. If you cannot afford to hire or make the correct costumes, you must give the audience a clear visual sign that you are representing, rather than reproducing, the clothes. To do this you must study the real thing, pick out one or two striking features such as a strap across the chest attached to the leather belt, a forage cap or a helmet. Use them with a basic costume of appropriate colour to produce your fighting force.

The chain mail and armour worn in the past creates a different, but equally knotty problem. It is best to concentrate on the headwear and weaponry. The tabard can alert the audience's imagination to conquering heroes, crusaders and jousting knights; the buff leather jerkin of the seventeenth century can be dressed with sashes, or belts and swords to cover the years of the late sixteenth and early eighteenth centuries. The bright red and blue tunics and cross belts of the nineteenth and the khaki of the twentieth centuries can be suggested with clothes of the same colour and accessories. The helmets and hats in all cases are a clear sign of battledress. Concentrate on recreating the silhouette. Flimsy and unconvincing helmets can be bought in fancy dress shops and strengthened with papier-mâché, and then

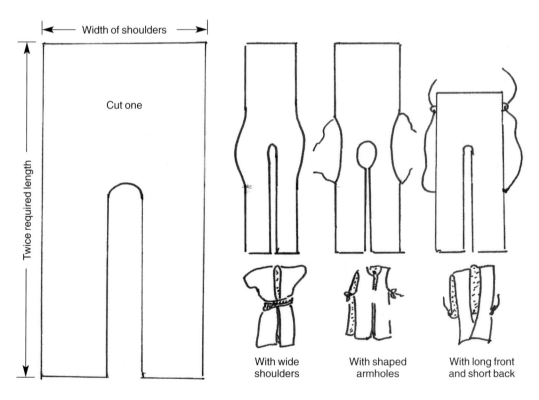

The tabard.

London street vendor wearing 'armour', home-made from old clothes, rags and belts. Photo: Hannah Bicât

painted in a more realistic manner. Shakos can be made of felt backed with stiffening.

It is not always necessary to create a fighting force that bears any actual relation to historical fact. An army will look like an army if the actors all wear black boots, carry black staves, and wear black balaclavas, provided they wear their costumes with conviction. A well stocked army surplus shop will have hats, protective helmets, belts and accessories which, even if they have to be painted to hide their modern khaki, will add a military feeling to the costume that the audience will recognize.

SUITS, COATS AND JACKETS

Fitted Doublets and Jerkins

There are not many modern clothes that can be adapted to the doublets and jerkins of the fifteenth- to seventeenth-century gentleman. Patterns for recreating correct versions of these garments can be found in the books recommended in the bibliography. Less complicated versions can be made using a pattern for a man's nightshirt or pyjama jacket: these are cut on simple lines that can be altered by the costume maker to suit the period. Use thick fabric that will hold its shape well, and note particular points such as cuff detail, sleeve shape, neckline, length and fullness. Aim to create an impression of the silhouette of the time, rather than a copy of the whole costume. If a sleeved garment is beyond your budget or capability, a better alternative may be a sleeveless jerkin or a waistcoat over a shirt, or even just a cloak or sash and hat worn with a basic costume. Consider using a tabard split down the front and belted; a couple of pleats stitched flat under the belt will make it lie more smoothly.

Eighteenth-Century Coats

There is no modern version of these knee-length and often full-skirted coats. They have to be made, and they use up a great deal of cloth. A modern jacket pattern that has seams down the side back, as well as the centre back, is the easiest to adapt, as the width and length of the coat skirts can be created by lengthening and widening those seams below the waist. An easier alternative is a long fronted waistcoat worn over a full-sleeved shirt; this is, of course, incorrect wear for an eighteenth-century gentleman, but when it is dressed up with good accessories it will give an impression of the time. This sort of simplification will only work if it is carried through in the clothes of all the characters – otherwise it will look as if the actor has forgotten to put on his coat.

Trousers

The difference in width of trouser leg between periods is obvious. False turn-ups can be created by running a 5mm (¼in) pin tuck round the trouser leg 3 or 4cm (1 to 1½in) from the bottom, and pressing it upwards to create a line of shadow onstage. A more difficult problem is the height of the rise – that is, the length from crotch to waist – which is lower in modern trousers than in the trousers of the past, which were meant to be worn with braces. Modern trouser patterns can be used, and the height of the rise lengthened. The width can be adapted to make baggy or tight breeches, leggings, tights and different types of trousers.

Breeches, Shorts and Knickers

Trousers can be cut off into breeches, and the knee-bands cut from the remnants. Measure the length over a bent knee or the actor will have difficulty sitting and kneeling. Leggings or tights can be chopped off short to make close-fitting underwear for men in short tunics. Underwear that shows should have the fly opening sewn up.

Suits, Coats and Jackets

Modern suits, or modern suit patterns, can be adapted to make them look more like suits of the twentieth century. The jacket can be given an extra button at the top, and the edges can be re-cut and braided. The jacket can be shortened and fitted more closely to the waist, and the fabric from the trousers unpicked and used to make tails or the bottom half of a frock coat. Many modern casual jackets or short coats are quite close in shape to the working clothes of previous centuries: do enough research to be sure of the styles you are trying to recreate, and search for clothes that are close in cut and fabric. Some modern women's coats and jackets, altered to fit the waist closely, can change their appearance completely when worn with an ankle-length skirt and period accessories. No alterations you can make will create a perfect result, but the silhouette, the hats, shoes and other accessories, will be the points that the audience notice most, and you can encourage them to do so with colour. Thus the shortcomings of your altered suit will not draw the eye if the jacket and skirt or trousers are a dark, unremarkable colour and the accessories are lighter coloured and interesting.

Waistcoats

Modern waistcoats and waistcoat patterns can be adapted in length and height of neckline to recreate those of other eras. An alteration as simple as ironing the points at the waist into a straight line and tacking them up will transform the line, and the addition of a shawl-type collar will make an even greater difference. The split-down-the-front version of the tabard can be cut waist-length at the back and long at the front, and secured round the waist with attached tapes.

Cloaks

A swirling cloak can be made from a circle of cloth shaped for the neck at the centre. A semi-circle will make a more restrained shape. A straight length of cloth, perhaps curved on the two front edges, can be held in place across the chest with cords or bands. A smaller cloak can be positioned over a larger one, and stitched into the collar as one to make a cape-collared cloak. Endless variations can be made on these basic themes. Some cloaks sit more securely if the shoulders are shaped with darts to the neck. A cloak that insists on slipping back can be secured with tapes that go under the armpits and tie invisibly underneath the folds of cloth at the back.

Robes

The difference between robes and cloaks is that robes usually have sleeves or slits for the arms to pass through. They are generally unfitted garments, and rely on the natural hang of the fabric to create an impression. The exceptions can be made from adapted patterns for jackets or dressing gowns. A long tabard can be used, or a T-shaped tunic can be split up the front as a basic shape and given collars, cuffs and so on, according to the design required.

ACCESSORIES

Ties and Cravats

Make good use of neckties and cravats: they may be small, but they create a powerful effect. The colour, pattern, texture, thickness, knot and neatness of a tie can convey so many messages about time and character. Think of the difference between the subtle silk tie elegantly emerging from an immaculate collar, and the knotted rag of a neckerchief crumpling out of a collarless shirt. Remember there is nothing to stop you tying a traditional tie in a bow if you chop off the wide end or conceal it beneath the waistcoat. The cravat, which made its first frilly appearance around the time of Charles II and has kept going in its various forms ever since, can be made from all sorts of scraps: lace-edged frills, long starched strips, soft satin folds, bright patterns and colours in silk, have all made an appearance over the centuries. The fabric of the wide end of a tie unpicked, opened out and pressed can be used to create a made-up cravat. So can mats and napkins, lace-edged runners, doilies, and even old stockings. Both cravats and ties can be made up and stitched, and fastened with hook-and-eye or Velcro at the back of the neck.

Aprons

These most adaptable and simply made accessories are of immense value to the period

Aprons and overalls.

costume designer, particularly when money and skilled cutters are not available. The apron – often little more than a flap of cloth on a waistband – covers a large portion of the front of the body cheaply and easily. Aprons can be delicate lace and silk ornaments on the eighteenth-century lady, or thick leather protection from the forge fire for the blacksmith. Short or long, flowery or starched white, they tell the audience about the life of the character. They can give shape to an unfitted dress, and stress the position of the waist as it goes up and down over the centuries.

Shawls, Scarves and Sashes

All of these can be used to give messages about the wearer to the audience, with a minimum of sewing. Remember when you are choosing the fabric that the material will be seen in folds, and not as a flat piece that alters, and in some cases destroys, the effect of a patterned cloth. Make sure that the actor knows how to wear or tie the cloth, and if necessary sew the folds into place to make it easier to wear.

Waistbands

A stiff, boned, shaped waistband can give shape and colour to a dress. It can also give the impression to both the audience and the actress who wears it, of a corseted body. The pattern can be adapted in width and size, but the fit should be very close. The waistband should dictate the shape of the waist.

DECORATION

Ribbon

Wide ribbon is a budget-gorging piece of haberdashery. Instead, try sewing tubes of any lightweight fabric of suitable colour and turning them inside out: in this way you can make perfectly successful ribbons, and wide ribbon, often with more body than the ribbon from a haberdasher, can be made cheaply. A strip of cloth, particularly a stiff satin or taffeta, frayed at the edges and zigzagged, produces an excellent effect.

Lace

Choose lace with a pattern coarse enough to show up from a distance. The shape of the edge should be clearly defined. Lace cloth can be cut with a strong zigzagged or scalloped edge that will show well onstage. The coarse, crocheted lace found on old tablecloths and runners produces an excellent effect.

Fringes and Tassels

Fringing and tassels of all sorts can be bought, but long fringe is very expensive. Coarse fringe and tassels can be made from fabric that does not fray, when several layers can be cut at once. This works particularly well when a stretch material is cut across the width of the cloth.

Braid

Take care that braid is not too heavy for the fabric, and that it lies smoothly, without rucking or stretching the cloth it is attached to: the stage lighting that shows up the braid so clearly also shows up the slightest wobbly line or puckered hem. Imagine what the trimming you are choosing will look like on stage; many bindings, stiffenings and tapes look better than trimmings designed for the purpose. Mock braid can be painted on the fabric. Check that masking tape doesn't mark the fabric if you use it to guide your lines.

Binding and Facing

Binding and external facing can be used as a decorative device to give a contrasting or clearly defined edge to clothes. It is much cheaper than braid, and can be quicker than hemming.

Tucks

Tucks, singly or in rows, are a cheap decorative finish for garments and have the advantage of adding body to the hem of a skirt, a sleeve or a blouse front. The lines of light and shadow created by tucks are exaggerated by the strong stage light.

Paint

Paint, dye and bleach can all be used to decorate clothes, shoes and hats, and can be combined with braid, sequins or other trimmings to add richness or age to costumes. Dye mixed as a strong solution, or bleach, can be stencilled or painted onto cloth, but test the effect on a scrap piece first to make sure it works as you want. Wash fabric after bleaching, or it will rot. The dye may run when washed. Special paints for cloth are available in art or craft shops, which will not wash out. Spray paint sold for cars comes in a huge range of colours and can be used with a stencil on small areas.

Stiffening Decorations

Ribbon, feathers, fabric flowers and small pieces of cloth can be coated with PVA glue and moulded into shape. The glue will not show when it is dry, and the decorations will retain the shape.

Dyeing

The dyes produced for home dyeing are easy to use provided you follow the instructions. Natural fibres will absorb dye easily, but some man-made fibres present more of a problem. If you are uncertain of the content of the fabric, boil up a sample in a small quantity of dye together with a scrap of washed white cotton cloth, and you will be able to gauge by their respective colours as the water heats up how successfully your cloth will take the dye. This is a very rough and ready guide to a huge subject.

Using Commercial Patterns

Most firms that sell dress patterns have a section in their pattern books for fancy dress. The patterns provide a way for those who have no experience or confidence in costume pattern cutting to make a garment that fits the actor and suits the period. When you look at the illustrations in these pattern books, take no notice of the picture other than to understand where the seams are placed: that is the information you are looking for and paying for. The obvious details of the design such as the colour, fabric and trimming, should be ignored. You are not designing a costume to make a splash at a party: you are creating a composite picture onstage, and the costume you make will probably be in heavier cloth and with subtler colour contrasts than the fancy dress costume in the picture. Do not be put off if the shape of the design is not exactly the same as your vision of the character: choose the closest you can find, and alter the details. Wedding dress patterns that are influenced by period costume are another useful source of patterns.

End Note

You could dress the mediaeval troubadour as a modern pop star, and though his songs might sound different, his body and the lyrics would be essentially the same. For the one, you might have to wait a year for the song, as the singer

The lyrics of two songs: 'A smile from your eyes is like paradise' from an eleventh-century troubadour song; and 'I'm in heaven when I see you smile', from a twentieth-century pop song show that love, at least, has not changed.

travelled on foot to your village; for the other, a touch of a finger will bring the song to your ear.

The apparently bewildering changes in fashion are really quite superficial because bodies and minds have changed so little in the last millennium. We still live and die, love and fight, have children and put on our clothes in much the same way. The clothes continue, as they always have and probably always will, to reflect the way humans see themselves, and the view of themselves they want to offer to their fellow humans. And actors still dress up and perform plays.

USEFUL TIPS FOR COSTUME MAKERS

1. A button covered in the same fabric as a dress will be a useful guide for an actress to find the correct place to hold up her skirt or train in order to keep her ankles covered.

2. A stiff tag for threading through eyelets can be created by coating the end of tape or ribbon with PVA glue and rolling it between the fingers. It will be firm when dry.

3. A ground-length skirt hem can be a little shorter at the front and dip at the sides and back to make walking and dancing easier.

4. A hidden belt loop at the side seams or back will make sure the belt is worn where it was designed to be worn.

5. A piece of cloth on a belt can represent the train of a skirt at rehearsals: everybody onstage will get used to not treading on it before the actress starts wearing the real costume.

6. A short piece of boning at the centre back of a collar that flops when it shouldn't will help it stand firm,

7. A small percentage of Lycra in cloth will save a great deal of ironing.

8. A strip of thin foam glued to the inside of a hat will stop it slipping about.

9. A tight belt or waistband can have an invisible 15cm (6in) of elastic in the back or the side seam to allow for the expansion of the ribs.

10. Always fasten Velcro before you wash a garment, or it may catch on cloth and damage it

11. A facing cut from a slightly heavier cloth on a full skirt will help it to hold its shape well.

12. A heavy skirt needs a firm, well-fitting waistband.

13. It is often useful to bind the low neck of a bodice and run a drawstring through it – it helps with last-minute adjustments to the shoulders and neckline.

14. Ask the actor at a fitting to sit down, stand up, raise the arms and then check that the costume still looks all right without inappropriate straightening and tugging it back into position. Tight-fitting costumes can end up in a real mess of ruckles.

15. Check that actors can raise their arms when wearing a close-fitting coat or bodice if their performance demands such movements.

16. Check that the soles of shoes and boots will look alright if actors have to kneel or lie down onstage.

17. Children cannot cope with tight, uncomfortable clothes or shoes, and their performance may suffer dramatically if they have to wear them.

18. The measurement round the ribs can increase dramatically when people sing.
19. Consider the character, period and height of the actor when deciding the length of a walking cane: it makes a big difference to the deportment.
20. Costumes cut for working characters will look more convincing if you allow for the movements of their trade.
21. Cut a cloak so that it distributes its weight in a balanced way. A cloak that slips and constricts the neck of an actor can be kept on with press studs on the shoulder, ties under the arms or a loop and tie at the back of the neck.
22. Cut and gather petticoats to echo the silhouette of the skirt.
23. Cut costumes with generous seam allowances and don't clip seams until after the fitting.
24. Don't cut backs too narrow or sleeves too tight. Actors of today need more freedom to move onstage than an authentically cut costume permits (and you can always take it in!)
25. Don't let actors wear boxer shorts under tight breeches or trousers – they wrinkle and look lumpy.
26. Every actor works best in comfortable and appropriate footwear.
27. Experiment with actors with their hairstyle before the rush of the dress rehearsal.
28. Find space at a final fitting for an actress to check she can walk with ease in her long skirt.
29. Folds and drapes in costumes can be arranged on the actor and secured into position with catch-stitches to tapes or a lining on the inside.
30. Great care should be taken that children's costumes are comfortable, or they won't be able to help fidgeting onstage.

31. Hatpins can be made with wire and sealing wax or beads.
32. If you have to create rags and tears, patches and marks of wear on a costume, imagine where they would occur in real life.
33. It helps actors a lot if you provide them with stand-in practice skirts, cloaks, trains, walking sticks, and so on, for rehearsal.
34. It is better, if possible, for actors to be able to fasten and unfasten their costumes without the help of a dresser.
35. It is expensive and time-consuming to knit period jerseys which can often be recreated from modern sweaters or sewn from jersey fabric. When altering a jersey, stitch before you cut.
36. If you make up the bow or knot on a garment or girdle and fasten it with a hook and eye you can make sure of the effect you want at every performance.
37. It is often necessary to cheat the brims of hats and bonnets so that they don't screen the face of the actor from the audience.
38. It seems to be true that most women do not object to wearing corsets but men find restrictive costume more difficult work in. This is a generalization but worth considering.
39. It will save trauma at the dress rehearsal if you always check at the fittings that actors can sit, kneel, squat or do whatever they have to onstage when wearing their costume.
40. Lacing is a most adjustable sort of fastening. So are tapes.
41. Leggings with a heel strap are easier to make than tights, and can be used when the feet do not show.
42. Let down a waistcoat at the shoulders if you need to cover a gap between waistcoat and trousers.

43. Linen is a beautiful fabric but can look dreadful onstage if it is not ironed perfectly. Creases are exaggerated by stage lighting,

44. Little girl's stage skirts should be supported on a light bodice or straps, or they will tend to slip down over their hips.

45. Make it easy with markings or press-studs to re-attach in the right place any light collars and cuffs removed for washing.

46. At a final fitting make sure that breeches' kneebands allow actors to sit and kneel.

47. Make sure before the dress rehearsal that hats stay on when they should and come off with ease and not too much hair ruffling.

48. Make sure bodices and skirts do not gape in the middle when an actress raises her arms or dances.

49. Make sure that boning on side seams doesn't dig into the armpit.

50. Make sure that hat decoration doesn't screen the profile from the audience – wire the spine of feathers if necessary.

51. Make sure that pockets are deep enough for their purpose but not to deep to be convenient.

52. Make sure that pockets don't turn themselves to the outside of a garment when used in a hurry onstage.

53. Make the waist of a petticoat slightly too large, so that it sits just below the natural waistline and does not increase the waist measurement.

54. Many modern clothes can be made into period clothes for poor characters. Start by ripping out interfacings and stiffening, and cutting the hems off. Then try to recreate a rough silhouette of the time. Use layers.

55. Many people object to the use of real fur onstage.

56. Many people today are unsure of the position of their waist and when sending measurements will measure below the waist. Ask them to measure at the narrowest point.

57. Necks expand when people sing or shout. Allow for this when you cut the collar.

58. Period costumes are heavy – make sure that coat hangers are up to the job.

59. Petticoats are never a waste of money – they improve the look of any skirt that would have been worn with one in the past.

60. Petticoats can be made of any cloth of appropriate weight, with a white cotton or appropriate frill or facing at the hem.

61. Props such as parasols, fans, bags, and so on, should have a loop so that they can be hung on the wrist and leave the hands free.

62. Provide underclothes that create the right shape of bosom for the period.

63. Quilt-stitch the wadding on padding so that it does not become displaced and lumpy in the wash.

64. Remember to allow a slit for the sword when cutting a coat that needs it.

65. Sew or glue hair ornaments or jewelled hair decorations onto hatpins or combs.

66. Shoelaces make excellent tie fastenings for kneebands, necks and wrists, as well as shoes. Flat ones are more secure than round ones.

67. Small children's stage trousers should be supported by braces rather than the waistband if you want them to stay up neatly,

68. Small costume props such as handkerchiefs or watches can add an aura of authenticity to the costume even if the are only seen and not used on stage.

69. Stockings worn with breeches should be gartered above the knee or there may be a gap below the kneeband.

70. Stop hoods slipping back with a small comb sewn inside.

71. Teach actors how to tie cravats, bows and ties in the correct knot.

72. Trousers flatter the leg if they are cut slightly longer at the back than at the front.

73. Trousers were ironed flat until about 1890 when they started to be pressed with creases front and back.

74. When choosing cloth for costumes consider the way they will be looked after in performance – some companies have a big wardrobe department with cleaning, washing and drying facilities while others have just one hardworking wardrobe mistress and a clapped-out washing machine.

75. When choosing cloth for period costume remember that the colour and pattern can be altered but there's not much you can do to change texture.

76. When cutting trousers for someone with a large stomach make sure you add extra length in the crotch-to-waist seam or there will be a gap between waistcoat and trousers.

77. When fastening a tight bodice work from the waist upwards, stop mid-way, ask the actress to position her bosom in the right place for the costume, and continue the fastening process to the top.

78. When fitting a tight bodice make sure the actress can take a breath deep enough to expand the diaphragm, or it may hamper her voice production.

79. Wigs should be kept on wig blocks in the dressing room – empty paint tins will do the job if you haven't the real thing.

80. It is pointless to pursue historical accuracy if the audience can't see its effect.

BIBLIOGRAPHY

Arnold, J. *Patterns of Fashion 1860–1920* (ISBN 0333136017)
Arnold, J. *Patterns of Fashion 1560–1620* (ISBN 0333382846)
Bicât, T. *Making Stage Costumes* (Crowood Press, 2001) (ISBN 1861264089)
Boucher, F. *A History of Costume in the West* (Thames and Hudson)
Buck, A. *Clothes and the Child 1500–1900* (ISBN 09035585294)
Doyle, R. *Waisted Efforts – An Illustrated Guide to Corset Making* (ISBN 09683033900)
Dryden, D. M. *Fabric Painting and Dyeing for the Theatre* (ISBN 0435086243)
Hibbert, C. *The Story of England* (Phaidon 2000) (ISBN 0 7148 8652 9)
Holkeboer, K. S. *Patterns for Theatrical Costumes* (ISBN 0896761258)
Motley *Designing and Making Stage Costumes* (ISBN 1871569443)
Nunn, J. *Fashion in Costume 1200–2000* (The Herbert Press, 2000) (ISBN 07136 50036)
Pratt, L. and Woolley, L. *Shoes* (ISBN 1851772855)
Strong, R. *The Spirit of Britain* (Hutchinson 1999) (ISBN 185681534X)
Swinfield, R. *Stage Make-up Step by Step* (ISBN 155870390X)
Thorne, G. *Designing Stage Costumes* (ISBN 1 86126 416X)
Turner Wilcox, R. *The Dictionary of Costume* (Batsford) (ISBN 071340856 1)
Waring, L. *Hats Made Easy* (ISBN 1863511504)
Waugh, N. *The Cut of Men's Clothes 1600–1900* (ISBN 0571057144)
Waugh, N. *The Cut of Women's Clothes 1600–1930* (ISBN 0571085946)

INDEX

anorak   111
apron   43, 59, 70, 71, 78, 85, 97, 100, 109, 130, 131
armour   32, 127, 128
audience   14

bag   43, 71, 96, 109
baldric   64
bare feet   71, 81, 89
baroque   45, 54
basic costume   11, 12, 14, 15, 17, 18, 49, 81
battledress   127
Bayeux Tapestry   21, 24
beard   38, 49
belt   30, 43, 85, 99
beret   93
Bible, Authorised Version   44
binding   132
blouse   96, 109, 120
blouse pattern   121
bodice   37, 38, 56, 57, 70, 81, 88, 123
bodice pattern   123
bonnet   26, 29, 43, 66, 69, 77, 79, 82, 87
boots   26, 69, 71, 81, 87, 94
boots, Chelsea   84
boots, skating   84
boots, Wellington   66, 75
braces   85, 99
braid   132
breeches   36, 41, 52, 56, 62, 71, 89, 129
brocade   55, 56
buckle   52, 57, 61
budget   15, 17, 18

bum-roll   125
bun   79, 91, 93, 106
bust improvers   88
bustle   125

Canterbury Tales   24
cap   47, 49, 57, 69, 71, 79, 84, 97
cap, baseball   109
cap, cloth   99, 109
cap, peaked   108
cape   70
catwalk fashions   104
cavalier   66
central heating   111
chain mail   9, 32, 127
Charles I   45
Charles II   54, 55
Charleston   90
chemise   76, 90
children's clothes   32, 43, 53, 64, 67, 87, 89, 100, 112
choker   94
Civil War   45, 46, 51
cloak   27, 30, 38, 41, 49, 52, 59, 62, 66, 70, 73, 82, 130
cloth   15, 21, 27, 40, 45, 49, 55, 65, 66, 69, 90, 111
clothes 'a l'anglaise'
coat   55, 56, 61, 66, 73, 82, 129
coat, morning   99
coat, short   75
codpiece   41
coif   26, 29, 32, 38, 43, 114
collar   43, 46, 51, 62, 66, 78, 85, 90, 91, 94, 120

comb   79
corset   20, 66, 70, 75, 76, 77, 82, 88, 89, 90, 91, 94, 114, 123
corset pattern   124
cotton   55, 56
cravat   55, 62, 73, 78, 85, 130
crinoline   76, 82
Cromwell, Oliver   45, 46, 54
curls   47, 57, 59, 66, 67, 69, 81

Dior, Christian   103
director   15
documentary   108
doublet   40, 41, 44, 51, 129
dresses   22, 35, 47, 48, 57, 67, 69, 70, 81, 108
dye   133

Edwardian   91, 96
Elizabeth I   34, 36, 44
Elizabeth II   91, 103
embroidery   56, 66
epaulettes   41

facial hair   16, 27, 82, 109, 114
facing   132
fans   38, 55, 57, 59, 71, 76
farthingale   36
feathers   57, 67, 69, 93
flat hat   40
flower   81
flying shuttle   55
fob watch   75, 87, 100
forearms   57
fringe   82
frock (coat)   62
frock coat   84
fur   34, 90, 96

gaiters   85
genre   14
girdle   22, 26, 27
gloves   32, 38, 43, 64, 71, 75, 76, 78, 87, 88, 96, 97, 100

Gothic   23
gown   40, 59
Great Fire of London   55
guillotine   65

hair   24, 27, 35, 38, 47, 49, 57, 61, 67, 71, 79, 82, 91, 97, 100, 106, 109, 114
hair accessories   79
hair dye   106
hairband   35
handkerchief   64, 100
hat   29, 32, 35, 38, 47, 67, 71, 78, 82, 87, 90, 106, 114–119
hat, boater   79, 84, 99
hat, bowler   82, 84, 91, 109
hat, felt   26, 29, 93
hat, lady's   93
hat, panama   99
hat, straw   26, 29, 57, 79, 93, 99
hat, tall   49
hat, top   71, 82, 97
hat, trilby   99, 109
Hawksmoor   55
headscarf   93
helmet   20, 127
Hennin   26, 35
Henrietta Maria   45
Henry VII   33
Henry VIII   16, 34, 36
high-crowned hat   40
high-street fashion   111
hippies   109
hood   29, 32, 35, 57, 75
hoop   59
hose   41

icon   35

jacket   51, 67, 73, 78, 82, 84, 90, 99, 105, 129
jacket, bomber   111
jacket, dinner   88, 100
jacket, sports   91, 111

INDEX

James I   44
jeans   9, 37, 85, 105, 111
jerkin   40, 44, 51, 129
jersey   91, 100
jewellery   32, 34, 38, 39, 59, 71, 87, 96
Jones, Inigo   45

knickerbockers   87, 89
knickers   76, 129

lace   34, 57, 59
lace   45, 46, 49, 51, 53
leg warmers   108
leggings   29, 30, 108
Liripipe   29
Livery   67, 87
logo   105, 108
loincloth   32

maid   78, 79
make-up   47, 57, 61, 79, 93, 96, 106,
    114
mills   65
mini-skirt   57
mittens   71
mobcap   79
mobile phone   112
mourning dress   78
moustache   49, 59, 71, 82, 88, 97
movement   17, 18
muff   55, 59, 66, 71, 75, 87
music   13, 44, 104

neckerchief   75, 85
new look   103
nightgown   37

overall   100, 109, 131
overcoat   66, 84
overtunic   70

padding   37, 45, 59, 88, 89
paint   133
painting   13, 44, 105

pantaloon   71
parasol   71, 76, 97
patches   57
patterns   12, 114, 133
patterns, dress   108
petticoat   59, 70, 76, 87, 90, 91, 125
photograph   10, 104
piercing   11
pinafore   75, 87, 102
plague, the   54
pocket flaps   61, 62,
portraits   10, 34, 37, 56
props   17
Puritan   45, 47, 49, 53

quotes   12

Raleigh, Sir Walter   41
renaissance   33
research   15
reticule   71
ribbon   57, 69, 81
ringlets   66, 67, 79, 81
robe   22, 35, 130
Rolex   41
round hat   61, 71, 84
roundhead   46
royal progress   34
royalist   46, 51, 53
rucksack   112
ruff   38, 43, 122
ruff pattern   123

sandals   109
sash   47, 51, 53, 64, 70, 75, 87
satin   55, 56
scarf   49, 59, 70, 112, 132
script   10, 14, 15, 20
set designer   15
Shakespeare   14
shako   125
shawl   66, 70, 75, 76, 81, 82, 132
shirt   41, 43, 53, 62, 78, 85, 99, 104, 111,
    120

shirt pattern   121
shirtsleeves   62
shoes   26, 29, 17, 35, 47, 51, 57, 61, 69, 71,
    87, 94, 108, 119–120
short-back-and-sides   97
shorts   102, 113, 129
side-whiskers   82
signs   10, 34
signs   18
silhouette   16, 46, 55, 57, 81, 88, 90,
    127
silk   34, 56
skirt   38, 55, 57, 66, 79, 81, 82, 90, 96, 97,
    104, 105, 108, 125
skirt patterns   126
skirt, circular   82
skullcap   40
sleeves   40, 41, 47, 59, 81
smock-frocks   62, 75, 85
smoking cap   61
socks   84, 102, 109
Spencer   70
spinning   65
Spinning Jenny   55
sportswear   78, 90, 108
status   10
stays   56, 59, 67, 89
stock   62, 73
stockings   29, 35, 47, 61, 69, 76, 81, 87, 93,
    94, 96, 104, 108, 119–120
suit   41, 44, 56, 62, 73, 91, 99, 104, 111,
    129
suit, Eton   87
suit, sailor   87, 89, 102
suit, skeleton   75
suit, tailored   96
sun glasses   109
sunbonnet   79
Sunday best   90
suntan   90
suspender belt   108
sweater   100, 111, 112
sweatshirt   111
sword   23, 55, 64, 127

symbol   35

tabard   30, 41, 70, 109, 125
tabard pattern   127
tailcoat, evening   85, 99, 100
tattoo   11
teenager   103
text   14
tie   85, 100, 112, 130
tie, bow   100, 112
tights   30, 41, 81, 87
train   90
trainers   81, 109
tricorn   57, 61
trouser suit   109
trousers   71, 73, 78, 82, 85, 90, 91, 99,
    105, 109, 125
T-shirt   37, 105, 109, 111, 112
tuck   133
Tudor   10, 33, 35, 37, 41
tunic   26, 29, 38, 39, 120
tunic pattern   121
turban   69, 93
tutu   20

umbrella   109
underclothes   81
underpants   41
undershift   37, 121
uniform   20, 67, 78, 84, 87, 90, 96, 105,
    109, 127, 128
uniform, school   9, 78, 87, 113

veil   24, 47, 79
velvet   34, 56
Venetians   41
Victoria   16, 76, 81
Victorian   77, 82

waistband   94
waistcoat   53, 56, 62, 66, 73, 78, 85, 91,
    99, 100, 130
walking cane   62, 75, 78, 87, 88, 100
weaving   65

wig   10, 55, 59, 61, 66, 67, 79
William the Conqueror   9, 21
wimple   24, 38
wireless   104
wool   34, 56

workclothes   10, 27, 32, 38, 43, 49, 53, 59, 62, 70, 75, 82, 84, 85, 94, 96, 97, 99, 100, 109, 112
World War II   96, 99, 104
wreath   35